THE
Gift of Health

THE
Gift of Health

The NHS, charity and the mixed economy of healthcare

Mark Lattimer

with contributions by
Karina Holly and Sari Kovats

A DIRECTORY OF SOCIAL CHANGE PUBLICATION

The Gift of Health
The NHS, charity and the mixed economy of healthcare
Mark Lattimer

with contributions by Karina Holly and Sari Kovats

Published by the Directory of Social Change,
24 Stephenson Way, London NW1 2DP, from whom
further copies and a full publications list may be obtained.

Designed and typeset by Kate Bass

Printed and bound by Page Bros., Norwich

British Library Cataloguing-in-Publication Data

A catalogue record for this book is available
from the British Library

ISBN 1 873860 32 3

Front cover photo: Robert Coultas,
© Barnaby's Picture library

The Directory of Social Change gratefully acknowledges
the assistance of the Baring Foundation in supporting the
research for this book.

To my father and mother
who served the NHS well

Acknowledgements

I would like to thank the following individuals and organisations for their help in the production of this book: Jean Gaffin of the National Hospice Council, Dr Richard Stone, Baby Life Support Systems (BLISS), the Independent Healthcare Association, and the staff of the central register of the Charity Commission, as well as the hundreds of other organisations that responded to our requests for information. I am also particularly indebted to Anne Mountfield and to David Carrington for their patience and good humour.

Contents

Preface

In Britain in 1996 a first-time mother looks down anxiously at her frail new-born baby, just one of the three quarters of a million babies delivered every year under the care of the National Health Service. As she gazes down at the hi-tech intensive care cot she is surprised to read on the plaque that it was donated by charity.

At the same time, in another part of Britain, a private patient arrives for his operation at an exclusive private hospital – and is surprised to discover that it is a registered charity. Elsewhere, a woman realises that she can no longer provide the nursing care needed by her disabled brother and entrusts him to the NHS – which pays for him to be cared for by a health charity. Elsewhere again, an NHS patient finds himself checked into a private hospital for his treatment while at the same time a private patient checks herself into an NHS hospital. Before they are discharged, both are given the opportunity to make a donation. Welcome to the mixed economy of healthcare.

The old certainties of state-dominated healthcare in Britain are collapsing. Up to a decade ago it was self-evident that the NHS paid and provided for all but a tiny fraction of the nation's healthcare needs. Private healthcare was supplementary and marginal, drawing its principal attraction from the standard of hotel services, rather than medical services, it was able to deliver.

Now the situations and relationships illustrated at the head of this page, although not the norm, are becoming increasingly common. But while the growth in importance of the private sector is widely documented, the pivotal role of charity in the evolving healthcare economy has been little discussed.

Section Two of this book considers the relationship, and substantial overlap, between the charitable and private sectors in both the purchasing and provision of healthcare, and the consequent effect on the NHS. Section Three looks at charities specifically as healthcare providers, often working in close partnership with the NHS, and Section Four discusses the future of the charitable endowments and other assets currently held by NHS hospitals. But the first section focuses on how charity and charitable money is playing a growing role in buying services for the NHS and for its patients.

Executive summary

The NHS reforms established an internal market in which NHS purchasers (health authorities and GP fundholders) bought care from NHS providers (principally NHS trusts). In the new mixed economy of healthcare in Britain, however, the provision of NHS services is increasingly being entrusted to charitable and private organisations. At the same time, NHS trusts are becoming dependent on charity to subsidise their services, and in a bid to boost income are investing substantial funds into establishing facilities for private patients.

Reliance on charity

- Charitable income to the NHS in the UK as a whole in 1994/95 is estimated at between £469 million and £553 million. Nearly all this money was dedicated to buying basic medical services, including medical equipment, hospital buildings and running costs. This income is in addition to the expenditure by charities on medical research in the UK, which totalled £385 million in 1994/95.

- NHS capital development has become particularly reliant on charity. Nearly ten per cent of NHS medical equipment by value was donated by charity in 1993, the last year for which comprehensive figures are available. The value of equipment held by NHS trusts and health authorities that had originally been bought by the NHS actually fell by six per cent between 1992 and 1995, while the value of donated equipment held by the NHS rose by 30 per cent over the same period. By 1995 total charitable assets in the NHS were equivalent to over nine per cent of the value of all assets held by NHS trusts and health authorities.

- Dependence on charity is also particularly acute in certain specialties, such as diagnostics, cancer medicine, and in the field of neonatal and paediatric care. One survey found that two-thirds of the equipment in NHS neonatal units was donated by charity.

11

Subsidising private patients

- The turnover of NHS private patient beds increased by 63 per cent over the three years following the establishment of NHS trusts. Private patients enjoy regular use of NHS facilities, including equipment donated by charity, and both NHS and charity funds have been used to invest in the expansion of private beds in the NHS.

- Thirty-seven per cent of private acute hospitals are registered as charities, entitling them to full exemption from corporation tax, income tax and capital gains tax and a mandatory four-fifths off their business rates. Despite these tax reliefs, a comprehensive survey of fees charged to patients in charitable hospitals found that they were on average higher than those charged in BUPA hospitals.

- It is estimated that the total value of these charitable benefits to private hospitals may exceed £35 million a year. If this is added to the value of the tax relief on private medical insurance introduced in 1990 – now worth £85 million annually – the total cost to the taxpayer of subsidising the private healthcare sector comes to over £120 million every year.

- Although they are rarely described as profits, large annual surpluses are frequently made by private charity hospitals and are used to invest in expanding their exclusive private facilities. Whereas the number of beds available in private hospitals as a whole increased by 73 per cent between 1980 and 1994, the total of NHS beds fell by more than a third over the same period.

Using charities to deliver NHS services

- Under the community care reforms, healthcare previously delivered by the NHS is increasingly being provided by charities. A survey undertaken for this report found that a third of service contracts held between charities and NHS bodies were for the care of persons leaving long-stay NHS hospitals.

- Over two-thirds of charities in the same survey reported that the contract payments they received from the NHS did not fully cover even their revenue costs. Approximately a third of respondents with contracts reported they used fundraising income to subsidise the NHS contribution, 30 per cent said they used volunteer work, and 16 per cent used a grant from another charitable source.

- Although NHS rules prohibit charging patients for part of the cost of their care, there are a growing number of instances of healthcare services delivered outside hospital where people are forced either to pay or to rely on charity to meet part of the cost. This covers services as disparate as home nebulisers for people with asthma, disability living aids and, most significantly, continuing care or rehabilitation for people leaving hospital.

- Proposals are currently being considered by the Department of Health to take Britain's senior hospital, St Bartholomew's in London, out of the NHS and turn it into a charitable foundation. This follows the precedent set by the Tadworth Court Hospital in 1984.

The cost for the NHS

- As well as being an unstable source of income, charitable giving is highly inequitable, heavily skewed to wealthier areas where people can afford to give more. The growing role of charities and private companies as providers of NHS acute and nursing home care, and the increasing reliance on charitable income in some specialties, are thus creating major discrepancies in both the level and quality of NHS services available across the country. Hospitals in London and some other wealthy metropolitan centres have in addition been able to use their access to charitable funds to lever out a level of major capital investment or ongoing revenue commitment from the NHS that would be denied to them under standard NHS financing procedures.

- Similarly, the requirement for hospitals to seek private financing for all new major capital schemes under the private finance initiative has applied a further skew to NHS capital investment, away from public healthcare priorities, and towards income-producing assets, including private patient units, retail outlets, patient 'hotels', and car parks.

13

- Experience from other countries, most noticeably the United States, suggests that healthcare systems based on a mixed economy of provision, far from lowering costs through competition, actually increase healthcare costs substantially by creating incentives for providers to try and make large surpluses. In the US, where healthcare is provided largely by private and non-profit providers, healthcare consumes 14 per cent of the gross national product. In the UK, where it is dominated by the National Health Service, healthcare is equivalent to just over six per cent of gross domestic product.

SECTION ONE

Overview

CHAPTER 1
CHARITY'S ROLE IN THE MODERN NHS

'Let me explain why I want your help. I can no longer raise funds for my charities by making cakes, sweets, marmalade, having coffee mornings, and sales in my house as I have done most of my adult life. Apart from being disabled with multiple sclerosis and asthma, and other medical problems, I recently have been in St George's Hospital Tooting, having had a major cancer operation, leaving me with a permanent colostomy. In no way am I telling you this for you to feel sorry for me, for eventually I will come to terms with this, as I have had to come to terms with many things...

'No; the reason I have told you about my recent operation, is because I was the first person in [my] ward at St George's Hospital to use a very sophisticated pain machine, it is called "Bard PCA – Patient Controlled Anglesia Machine". These machines have proved so useful in the post operative field that more are planned for other wards. Of course they are very expensive between £1,500 and £2,000 each, and they have only ten in the hospital, five bought by the NHS.

'I could not have had better medical attention anywhere, and I was an NHS patient. I had this machine for three days whilst in the intensive care unit, and for two days on the ward. It gave me tremendous relief from the pain, on top of what the nursing staff were giving me by injections, and helped to get me through this very traumatic experience. I am sure that many more people could benefit with far less pain after major surgery, if more machines were available. But unfortunately cost is the problem.

'This is really why I am writing to you, in case there may be the possibility of your charity being able to help in any way... I always feel that "If the wish can be willed, then the means usually follow."

'I would then feel that I had done all I could to repay the Hospital for what they have done for me.'

This letter was received recently by a small charitable trust in London. It is just one of tens of thousands of letters seeking to raise money for the National Health Service sent to charities and other potential donors every year.

Many of these letters, as the one above, are written by patients or by patients' relatives. Many others come from consultants or doctors raising funds for their particular unit or specialty. Increasingly, appeals are also launched by hospital managers, often with the appeal letters signed by famous or distinguished patrons they have garnered for the cause.

And occasionally, charitable appeals are launched by the Secretary of State for Health. A new appeal to expand the internationally renowned Bloomfield Centre at the Lewisham and Guy's Mental Health NHS Trust was formally launched in October 1994 by the then Secretary of State, Virginia Bottomley. She said in her speech: 'The Bloomfield Centre is a truly remarkable place. Since opening 15 years ago it has combined excellence in teaching and research with high quality mental health services for local people. The new £0.9 million appeal I am launching today to extend the Centre, and enable the Bloomfield Learning Centre to provide bursaries for children whose parents cannot afford to pay for treatment [sic], will help this partnership go from strength to strength. I am pleased to announce that the Trust has already contributed £100,000...' (Department of Health, 94/467).

NHS fundraising has in fact already entered its second generation. For several years running, hospitals have topped the 'legacy league' compiled by Smee and Ford, a firm that monitors legacies for charities, with the number of bequests for each of 1994 and 1995 hovering around the 6,000 mark. The time of the one-off appeal started by the grateful patient is already passing, replaced by permanently staffed appeal charities looking to meet the ongoing needs of the local NHS. The following is from a letter written by a 'Fundraising Manager' based at the Royal South Hants Hospital.

'During the past ten years the Wessex Cancer Trust has been involved in many aspects of cancer care. We have recently helped to fund a new children's ward, the Piam Brown Ward, at Southampton General Hospital at a cost of £500,000. Another major commitment was the purchase of five mobile breast screening units for women, at a cost of £200,000, which will be of great benefit in the early detection of breast cancer. Our direct family support grants are increasing every month. We help with telephone bills, heating costs, travel and even a last holiday for some patients and their families.

'Now we have a new appeal. We urgently need to raise £300,000 to refurbish, extend and improve the Wessex Radiotherapy Centre at the Royal South Hants Hospital in Southampton. I do hope that you will be able to help us in some way...'

To the extent that these charitable appeals are evidence of a genuine shortfall in NHS provision, the quantity and range of the requests are alarming. Everything from preventative medical programmes to high technology clinical treatments to equipment for emergency and intensive care services can be found on the fundraisers' shopping lists. Many of these lists come with a price tag of millions of pounds.

Fundraising does not stop once a piece of equipment has been bought or a new NHS ward or unit built. Appeals for complex items of equipment now routinely seek to raise not just the purchase price but also installation and ongoing maintenance costs. The same goes for entire hospital units. The Wolfson Children's Cancer Unit at the Royal Marsden Hospital was built and equipped in 1993 with £4.5 million from the Royal Marsden Cancer Appeal, which raised a total of £25 million. Named after a large donor, the unit is now the subject of an ongoing appeal to help fund the research and specialist staff training required for its work.

For those brought up on the notion that the creation of the NHS in 1948 eradicated all class or income barriers to decent healthcare, it is particularly disturbing to note the frequency with which appeals cite individual lack of means as an obstacle to accessing services. (This is apparent in two of the examples quoted above.) The Mid Sussex Zipper Club is a cardiac patients support group which has raised over £35,000 since its formation in 1988, the money being used mainly to buy equipment for local hospitals, health centres and the ambulance service. One of the club's appeal letters begins: 'Have you, your family or any member of your staff suffered a serious heart attack or had open heart surgery?'.

The letter goes on to relate: '...perhaps when the patient cannot manage the journey unassisted, the club may be able to organise or provide transport to and from the hospital. The cost of a round trip to King's College Hospital is at least £30 but could be as high as £150 if a private ambulance is necessary. The Zipper club could help with the cost, or if there is financial hardship, could possibly cover the whole cost'. The shopping list enclosed with the appeal letter duly runs from an ECG machine for a medical centre, to a defibrillator unit and a pulse oximeter for the local ambulance emergency service, to £1,000 to cover 'Transport for heart patients'. Fundraisers, naturally, will do all they can to emphasise the urgency of their cause, but the reader is left with the firm impression of a National Health Service that is struggling to meet the existing levels of healthcare need and in particular to fulfil its duty to those who are less well-off.

The health needs that appear most urgent or vital are also the ones that the public feels most strongly should fall within the responsibility of the National Health Service. Many appeals address this issue directly and explain up front that the proposed service or equipment is not covered by the NHS, usually because of lack of resources. Thus one charity set up in the early 1990s called THRIVE ('Towards Healthier Rochdale Infants Vital Equipment') was registered at the Charity Commission with the following object: 'To relieve sickness by the provision of equipment for the maternity, gynaecology and childcare wards and units of Rochdale hospitals not available to them from statutory sources'.

A new phenomenon is the NHS appeal that complains not about the lack of statutory funding for a facility, but the lack of charity funding. The Royal Free Hospital in North London was founded in the Victorian era as a charity hospital to provide, as its name suggests, free healthcare to the poor and those who could not afford doctors' fees. For the last half century it has also been an example of modern NHS care at its clinical best. An appeal to establish a gastrointestinal diagnostic unit was launched in 1994 under the auspices of the hospital's school of medicine.

The appeal's treasurer argues: 'Most people are unaware that cancer of the colon is the second commonest cancer in the United

Kingdom and currently accounts for nearly 20,000 deaths per year. Most people are also unaware that if it is diagnosed and treated at an early stage, the outlook can be improved dramatically with 90 per cent of patients alive and well five years later'. The funding of the necessary diagnostic equipment, however, 'is hampered by the limited interest that a "bowel disorder" appeal generates amongst charitable bodies and individuals who are non-sufferers. Nevertheless, the need for such funding is as great as that for the more popular causes'. A century after its establishment, treatment at the Royal Free appears once again to be dependent on the vagaries of charitable fashion.

As well as supplying the necessary funds to provide healthcare to all, free at the point of delivery, the creation of the National Health Service was expected to deliver a rationally organised system of services driven by healthcare need rather than fashion, pity or the 'popularity' of some causes over others. Appeals like that for the Royal Free's gastrointestinal unit, therefore, cannot but raise serious questions for the planning of a system of health services that is increasingly turning to charity. This is discussed at more length in chapter 2. First we need to ask, exactly how much money does charity contribute to the NHS every year?

Annual NHS income from charity

Calculating a precise figure for the NHS's charitable income is not an easy task. Firstly, charitable funds enter the NHS through a number of different routes.

Donations made directly to a hospital or other unit will normally be paid into the charitable trust funds held by the relevant NHS trust or health authority. However, much NHS fundraising is now undertaken through separate appeal charities, giving each appeal an individual identity or public relations profile and keeping its funds separate from other charitable income intended for the same hospital or unit. In March 1996 there were 2,318 such appeals registered with the Charity Commission. Finally, donations, particularly of assets, can also be credited directly to the main accounts of the NHS trust or health authority. This is what would normally happen if, say, a league of friends purchased a new scanner for a hospital. Given these different routes and varying methods of accounting for charitable inputs to the NHS, it is important to avoid double-counting in any calculation of total charitable income.

The gradual shift in control of hospitals and provider units from health authorities to the newly-created NHS trusts throughout the early 1990s (with the concomitant annual exodus of these hospitals from the health authorities' books) has added further difficulties in tracking charitable income over time.

But changes to NHS accounting practice since the reforms also mean that for the first time it is possible to obtain accurate information on the value of equipment and assets donated to the NHS, as well as cash. Prior to 1991, the accounts of health authorities were drawn up on a revenue only basis, so it was impossible to quantify accurately the value of additions to capital assets. But the reforms introduced a new system of accounting for the use of capital in the NHS. All authorities and NHS trusts now have to record at current value the assets they hold and depreciate them over their working lives in their accounts. A distinction is made between assets purchased by the NHS (on which NHS trusts are liable to pay interest and dividends to the government) and donated assets.

Figures on charitable income revealed in the NHS accounts for England for each of the four years between 1991 and 1995 are given in the table. Separate totals are listed for: income to the charitable trust funds held by NHS trusts and health authorities; contributions to expenditure and donations of assets to NHS trusts; contributions to expenditure and donations of assets to health authorities. When interpreting the figures it is important to bear in mind the shift in control of hospitals and other units from health authorities to NHS trusts over the period: the NHS trust figures for 1991/92 relate to the 57 first wave trusts, the 1992/93 figures encompass a further 99 second wave trusts, the 1993/94 figures include a further 141 third wave trusts, and the 1994/95 figures include a further 127 trusts in the fourth wave, making a total of 419 trusts in that year.

Charitable income to the NHS (England) 1991 – 1995

	1991/92 £000	1992/93 £000	1993/94 £000	1994/95 £000
NHS trusts				
Contributions to expenditure	3,551	22,358	17,404	23,102
Donations of assets	19,381	48,456	59,376*	92,580*
Total	22,932	70,814	76,780*	115, 682*
Health authorities				
Contributions to expenditure ◆	10,641	9,059	13,671	6,802
Donations of assets	76,498	66,971	35,213	2,021
Total	87,139	76,030	48,884	8,823
Total (NHS trusts and authorities)	**110,071**	**146,844**	**125,644***	**124,505***
Charitable trust funds held by NHS trusts and health authorities				
Subscriptions and donations	111,254	105,833	114,094	111,522
Legacies	26,810	30,714	29,229	37,862
Income from investments & property	70,859	70,086	64,445	68,577
Income from fundraising	7,377	10,609	9,532	8,030
Other income	23,210	38,770	27,737	29,711
Total (charitable trusts funds)	**239,510**	**256,012**	**245,032**	**255,702**

* *Due to a change in accounting practice, the figures for donations of assets for 1993/94 and 1994/95 only reflect the increase in the current valuation of assets held due to the receipt of donated assets during the year. This figure is likely to be substantially less than the full value of assets donated in the year (see text).*

◆ *Contributions to the expenditure of DMUs (or provider units directly managed by the health authorities).*

SOURCE: NHS ACCOUNTS 1992-1995

To reach a figure for the total charitable income to the NHS it is not safe simply to sum the totals for trust fund income on the one hand, and NHS trust and health authority income on the other, as there is a danger of double counting assets that are bought with charitable trust fund income and then donated to an NHS unit. As charitable trust fund income is typically used to buy goods directly for the NHS, this is only likely to apply in the case where the same transaction is recorded as both capital expenditure in the trust funds' account and additions to donated assets in the NHS trust or health authority accounts.

The charitable trust funds' contributions to hospital capital expenditure were recorded in the 1994/95 accounts as worth £35.3 million. This figure would also be expected to include, however, a large number of capital purchases that fell below the capitalisation threshold in the NHS accounts of £5,000, as well as larger assets in respect of which the trust funds continued to hold the title, neither of which would then figure in the NHS trust or health authority accounts.

Potentially more significant than the transactions that may figure both in the charitable trust fund accounts and the main accounts, however, are the categories of charitable donation that do not appear anywhere in the NHS accounts. This includes donations of assets individually valued under the £5,000 capitalisation threshold (this would cover many of the items mentioned in the appeals above, from anglesia machines to ECGs to pulse oximeters); gifts of permanent endowment which are not recorded in the charitable trust funds income account; and, most importantly of all, income to the large number of appeals and funds that are maintained by individual consultants or nursing staff, either under the auspices of a hospital medical school or unofficially as a local initiative to benefit a particular ward or unit.

This latter category may be very large indeed. Anecdotal evidence from hospital managers and clinical staff suggests that in some hospitals there are many separate funds outside the control – or the knowledge – of the hospital management. One manager employed by an NHS trust in 1991 to undertake an audit of these charitable appeals explained: 'It was like peeling back the layers of an onion – we kept uncovering more and more charitable funds' (Lattimer and Holly, *Charity and NHS Reform*, DSC, 1992). And whereas the proceeds of the separate appeals launched by the hospital management itself will eventually show up in the accounts of the relevant NHS trust or health authority, most of these unofficial appeals launched by an individual clinician will not.

Finally, there is one additional factor which also indicates that the figures on charitable income recorded in the 1994 and 1995 NHS accounts significantly underestimate the real total. From 1994, figures for additions to donated assets are not separately recorded in the published NHS trust accounts. There is only a figure representing 'Increase in the donation reserve due to receipt of donated assets' (the donation reserve is a book-keeping figure used to calculate the current value of, and depreciation on, assets acquired through donation). The equivalent figure in the 1993 accounts is £21.7 million, considerably less than the total of additions to donated assets in 1993, which was £48.5 million. This suggests that there was at least this degree of under-estimation in the accounts for the following two years. However, between 1992 and 1993, the only two years for which the full figures were published, there was a rise of over 20 per cent in additions to donated assets held by both NHS trusts and health authorities. If such a rate of increase continued the following two years (not an unreasonable assumption given the explosion in NHS fund-raising), the figure for additions to donated assets in 1995 would have been much greater at £167 million, some £73 million more than the total recorded in the table above.

Taking into account only the degree of known under-estimation in the published NHS accounts and the need to make an allowance for any double-counting, the total charitable income to the NHS in England in 1994/95 is estimated at between £380 million and £448 million. These figures do not make any allowance for the value of charitable income to the NHS from unofficial appeals or those carried out under the auspices of hospital medical schools, and therefore may themselves under-estimate the true total.

Extrapolating from the England figures, this would put charitable income to the NHS in the UK as a whole in 1994/95 at between £469 million and £553 million. This is in addition to the expenditure by charities on medical research in the UK that year, which totalled £385 million (see chapter 2).

This is consistent with the results of an earlier Directory of Social Change study published in 1992. That study estimated charitable income to the NHS in 1991 at £360 million, based on the accounts of NHS charitable trust funds supplemented by survey data *(ibid.)*.

The other key finding of the 1992 study was that the role of charitable income in the NHS had shifted over the previous decade from paying for extras and additional services to paying for services that were part of the core responsibilities of the NHS. 'The role of charity in the NHS has altered fundamentally, with charity now being called on to fund major capital projects and also basic medical services. In the past charitable income has only had a very small peripheral part to play in the NHS, concentrating on providing small comforts for patients and staff and supporting research and the development of new treatments. However, the former consensus, that charity should not pay for the costs of core services that were the proper responsibility of the state, has now all but collapsed' *(ibid.)*.

The evidence presented above indicates that this process has continued apace, and that charity has spread from the day room and the laboratory and is now equally at home in the emergency room, the operating theatre and the intensive care unit.

Donated assets & capital development

Most of the hospitals or buildings used by the NHS are decades old, and many date from the last century or even before. From the patient's point of view, the provision of first-class services takes precedence over the fabric of the buildings in which those services are delivered. For the managers of NHS trusts, whose responsibilities cover both direct patient care today and the maintenance and investment needed for patient care tomorrow, the decisions on what takes priority are not so easy. One alternative, for those who have a sufficiently popular cause to sell, is to turn to charity for their capital investment needs.

The Jack and Jill Appeal was launched in 1996 by the

Frenchay Healthcare NHS Trust in Bristol. The simple appeal brochure is headed '2,327 reasons why Frenchay Hospital, Bristol needs a new Children's Unit' and goes on to explain: 'In 1995, 2,327 seriously ill children were admitted to Frenchay Hospital. Frenchay has a worldwide reputation as a centre of excellence for the treatment of children with severe burns, head injuries and neurological disorders... It's alarming to think that more children in this country die each year as a result of severe accidents than from cancer. That's why it's so important for Frenchay to carry on with its work as a national leader, providing specialist care for children suffering from serious accidents. But to carry on effectively, we need to raise £2 million to build and equip the new Children's Unit.'

The appeal describes in more detail why the current facilities are inadequate: 'The wards we currently use for children are hopelessly old-fashioned, quite unsuitable and expensive to run. They were built in the first half of the century and are laid out in the old style, which gets in the way of effective, modern nursing care. And that's not all. The two wards we use for children are at different ends of the hospital, so we have to duplicate specialised nursing care and equipment. Not only that but the simple geography makes it difficult, if not impossible, for neuro and plastic surgeons to work together effectively. The facilities for staff are far from adequate and the only route to the plastic theatres is via covered walkways exposed to the worst of the weather.'

At the Whittington Hospital in north London, half of the 400 beds are in Victorian buildings. Baroness Hayman, who chairs the Whittington Hospital NHS Trust, recently commented: 'The NHS has a horrendous backlog of repairs and maintenance problems. You are faced with all sorts of dilemmas. Do you carry on pouring good money after bad to try and prop up these buildings a few more years? Is it worth it? Or do you divert the money into patient care and just hope you will receive the authority for new buildings?' (*Observer* 10.3.96).

Until now that authority, and more importantly the funds to go with it, has rarely been forthcoming. A high proportion of the handful of major hospital redevelopment schemes that were given the go-ahead between 1985 and 1995, including developments at Great Ormond Street, the Royal Marsden, Guy's, and the Royal

Hospital for Sick Children in Edinburgh, had only managed to secure Department of Health backing through raising large amounts of matching funds from charity. The launch of the Private Finance Initiative, discussed in chapter 3, promises to release a wave of new capital investment in the NHS, but only for very particular kinds of scheme.

The situation regarding medical and other equipment in the NHS is even more pressing than it is for buildings. Larger or more complex items of medical equipment typically have a working life of between five and 15 years. Technological advances or innovations in clinical practice, however, mean that some items become outdated well before the end of their working lives. But for hospital managers working within very tight budgets and anxious to keep services running at full capacity, the temptation to postpone the replacement of ageing equipment is obvious.

The value of equipment held by NHS trusts and health authorities that had originally been bought by the NHS actually fell by six per cent between 1992 and 1995. Yet over the same period, the value of donated equipment held by the NHS rose by 30 per cent, the NHS accounts reveal (see graph).

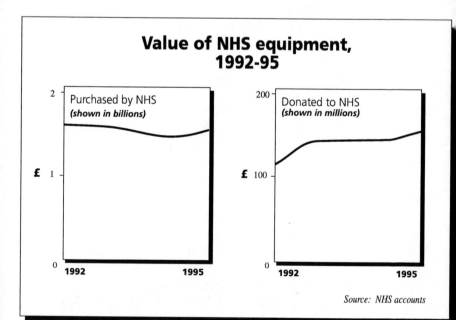

Source: NHS accounts

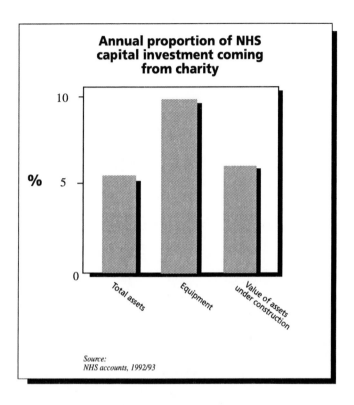

Annual proportion of NHS capital investment coming from charity

Source:
NHS accounts, 1992/93

Full figures for additions to donated assets were only published up to the 1993 NHS accounts, before a change in accounting practice ensured that such information was not collected separately. The 1993 accounts do, however, present a worrying snapshot of the extent to which capital development in the NHS has become reliant on charity (see bar-chart). Of the total value of assets acquired by the NHS in 1992/93, exactly six per cent came from charity. But taking equipment alone, the proportion acquired from charity is nearly ten per cent. In addition, donated assets accounted for over 6.5 per cent of the value of assets under construction in 1993.

The table below gives the total value of charitable assets held by the NHS for the five years from 1991 to 1995. This includes the donated assets held directly by NHS trusts and health authorities, together with the assets held by the charitable trust funds in the NHS.

Charitable assets in the NHS (England) 1991 – 1995

	1991 £000	1992 £000	1993 £000	1994 £000	1995 £000
NHS trusts:					
total donated assets	97,087	109,514	207,037	338,850	537,155
Health authorities:					
total donated assets	199,430	247,339	262,343	231,549	32,552
Charitable trust funds:					
total assets	683,365*	705,500*	880,347	1,039,338	1,386,968
Total	**979,882**	**1,062,353**	**1,349,727**	**1,609,737**	**1,956,675**

* Includes stock market investments listed at book value
Source: NHS accounts

The figure of nearly £2 billion for total charitable assets in 1995 includes investments held by the charitable trust funds recorded at market value, but also substantial property holdings that are still valued at cost. The fact that this property generated a net income of £21 million in 1994/95 suggests that it is worth rather more than its balance sheet valuation of £144 million. In fact the trust fund holdings include property occupying prime sites in central London, but only valued at historic cost.

The book value alone of the charitable assets held within the NHS rose by a staggering 56 per cent over the four years from 1991 to 1995 (doubling in market value). By 1995 total charitable assets in the NHS were equivalent to 9.2 per cent of the value of all assets held by NHS trusts and health authorities. It is clear that charity's role in NHS capital development, and in investing in the future of the NHS, is much greater than has hitherto been recognised.

Charity's wider NHS role

The financial contribution that charity makes to hospitals and other NHS units is not its only role in the Health Service. For many years charities have had a wider part to play in partnership with the NHS and one that has developed significantly in the 1990s.

The St John Ambulance and the British Red Cross have traditionally supplied a trained ambulance reserve service which can be called upon to support NHS ambulance services when confronted with a major incident or other unusual occurrence. They are also a familiar sight at sporting venues, fetes and other public events.

For the first time in 1993, the Department of Health published national guidelines placing many of the informal arrangements that had existed between the NHS Ambulance Service and the charity reservists onto a formally recognised basis. A letter from the NHS Executive to NHS ambulance chiefs explained: 'Whilst there is no compulsion to form a reserve, it is anticipated that this national initiative will act as a stimulus to services to review arrangements at local level. It is hoped that the reserves will create a cadre of trained St John Ambulance and Red Cross personnel with additional experience and familiarity with the operating procedures of NHS Ambulance Services; thereby allowing them to provide disciplined and integrated assistance in any major accident situation.' At the launch of the initiative the health minister added: 'This will enable reservists to undertake a number of important tasks and provide routine support to release ambulance personnel to undertake emergency duties'.

The guidelines themselves were drawn up jointly by the Association of Chief Ambulance Officers and the St John Ambulance and British Red Cross. The health minister's reference to 'routine support' notwithstanding, the charities were at pains to emphasise the limitations on their role, and this is reflected in the text of the guidelines: 'The principal purpose of establishing a reserve is to support the statutory services in the event of a major incident or other unusual occurrence. Therefore, reservists should not be called upon to provide normal ambulance service cover, or used as an alternative to increased expenditure by the

Ambulance Service, or to replace services withheld due to financial considerations. ... During any period of industrial dispute affecting the Ambulance Service, the role of the reserve shall be limited to providing support in the event of a major incident only' (*Ambulance Reserve Guidelines*, July 1993, Department of Health).

Another group of charities that have traditionally worked to complement the NHS are the leagues of hospital friends and the Women's Royal Voluntary Service. As well as raising money for hospitals, some of it through running tea-bars and small shops for patients and visitors, volunteers from these charities have performed a valuable function running hospital library and transport services and often simply befriending patients, particularly those in longer-stay beds.

Over time, however, the efforts of the leagues of friends and WRVS have been increasingly channelled into fundraising. There has also been rising concern over the types of requests the volunteers receive from hospitals, prompting the WRVS in 1994 to conduct a review of its giving policy to the NHS. The director of hospital services at WRVS commented: 'It is a cause for concern to us that donated funds are requested by hospital administrators for the purchase of certain items which fall within the hospital's statutory budget provisions, for example, legally required safety equipment for a paramedic team' (*Third Sector* 4.11.93).

Perhaps the most valuable services provided by charities and voluntary groups are those which the state could not itself provide, because they depend on features unique to the voluntary sector. This would include the self-help groups, generally for people with a particular medical condition and their relatives, providing information, counselling, patient advocacy and mutual support. There are literally hundreds of such groups, from the Alzheimer's Disease Society to the Zito Trust. The voluntary sector also has specific advantages in the community health field, where local community-based groups are well placed to build health awareness, tackle social or environmental factors conducive to poor health, and improve access to NHS services.

The Department of Health has a long-established programme of support for voluntary groups providing precisely such patient-led or community-based services, making grants under Section 64 of the Health Services and Public Health Act 1968. A key part of the government's early approach to the fight against AIDS was to provide support to charities such as the Terrence Higgins Trust which were considered more effective in reaching at-risk groups and providing appropriate services than a public authority would have been. Similar thinking lay behind the launch in the early 1990s of 'specific' or ring-fenced grants for voluntary groups working in the areas of mental illness and substance misuse.

Health alliances between different services and between the statutory, voluntary and private sectors are a central theme in the government's Health of the Nation initiative. At the 1995 Health Alliance Awards the winners included: the Ageing Well Project, organised by the charity Age Concern, which consists of nine pilot projects to promote better health for older people, including the recruitment of senior health mentors; and the Yellow Brick Road scheme in the North East, which brings together community groups to promote health for young people with measures that are both fun and educative.

A capacity to innovate is in fact something on which the voluntary sector has long prided itself. A range of innovations in NHS services, from sitting schemes for mentally ill people, to hospital at home schemes, to palliative care for the terminally ill, has been pioneered by the charitable sector over the years.

Praising the work of the outreach cancer nurses known as 'POONS', junior health minister John Bowis outlined in 1994 what could be described as the classic pump-priming role of charities: 'This is another example of the very productive relationship the NHS has with the voluntary sector. The Cancer Relief Macmillan Fund and Cancer and Leukaemia in Childhood blazed the trail in introducing Paediatric Oncology Outreach Nurse Specialists in specialist children's hospitals. The NHS is picking up some of the funding in this area... This in turn enables the charities to move into new areas' (Department of Health 94/341).

This pump-priming role is now very much the exception to the norm, however. Government encouragement for the development of a mixed economy of healthcare and the contracting out of health and community care services have given the charitable sector for the first time a major role in the provision of mainstream statutory services. Chapter 5 describes how charities are increasingly being used to provide, and to subsidise, services which were previously delivered by the NHS.

The community-friendly credentials of the voluntary sector have ensured that charity now even has a role in that last bastion of NHS provision: primary healthcare. As part of the reorganisation of health services in London, the Department of Health launched a programme of development for general practitioner and district nursing services within a designated London Initiative Zone (LIZ). Announcing as part of the initiative a fund of £7.5 million which would be available to support voluntary sector projects between 1993 and 1996, the then health minister Brian Mawhinney said: 'It is our intention that successful schemes will make a practical difference to the use of hospital beds in London. I want to see the build up of community based projects which will either enable prompt discharge of patients when there is no clinical need for them to remain in hospital or prevent hospital admission in the first instance. In this way beds can be freed up for those whose need is more urgent and waiting times in London will come down.'

As always, however, charity is called on to foot part of the bill. One of the earlier LIZ projects to go ahead, a 'healthmobile' to deliver primary care in Croydon to people who had difficulty in attending existing health centres, was launched in September 1994 by Mawhinney's successor as minister for health, Gerald Malone. Of the £75,000 cost of the project, £20,000 had come from local fundraising.

THE PLANNING DEFICIT

State central planning has gone out of fashion. The demise of Soviet-style communism has comprehensively discredited the economic model of state centralism. Fuelled by the new economic orthodoxy and fired by the Bretton Woods institutions, liberalisation measures have spread in countries across the globe, attesting to faith in the power of private competition rather than state control as the engine for growth. In Britain over the last decade, the active distaste for state control has boosted the role of the private sector in local authority services and the prison service, championed private control in the running of the great utilities and introduced a competitive quasi-market in the National Health Service.

But centralised planning has always held one great advantage for governments: a very high level of control. The implementation of the NHS reforms has thus been marked, at both national and district level, by a struggle between the local independence believed to boost output and quality, and the degree of central control necessary to a service where lives are at stake and where the everyday business failures that are an inevitable feature of the private sector would be simply unacceptable.

Within this rubric, the increased importance of charitable finance and of voluntary and private providers in the NHS presents a serious challenge to the planning function. Indeed, the charity sector's contribution to the NHS has exposed what could be termed a planning deficit in the service.

Charity, typified in public imagination by the spontaneous gift, is a planner's nightmare. The nightmare has two distinct, but inter-related, themes: insecurity and inequity. Firstly, charity is an intermittent and inherently unreliable source of support.

- The charitable income received by the NHS as a whole fluctuates considerably from one year to the next, although currently within the context of a general steep upward trend.
- The charitable income received by individual NHS Trusts, authorities and other units varies even more widely. This is

partly due to the planned cycle of major appeals, but also to the uncoordinated nature of much NHS fundraising and, more generally, to its patchy success.

- The highly politicised context in which change takes place in the NHS is unlikely to leave unaffected public support for NHS fundraising in the NHS. The uncertainty following the London Review, for example, might be expected to cause a big dent in charitable donations to hospitals in London (see chapter 7).

- Charities providing services under contract to the NHS are typically small organisations (by public sector standards) with a number of different sources of income, reliant on the drive and managerial ability of a few individuals. The financial stability of such organisations is often low, and their rate of turnover high.

Secondly, unless it is specifically targeted on the poor, charity often demonstrates a natural bias toward the better off. This may at first seem strange, but the logic is quickly grasped when one considers that rich communities can afford to give much more, and that most charitable giving is highly parochial (that is, donations tend to benefit the communities from which the donors come).

- Patients, ex-patients, their families and friends are for most hospitals probably the greatest potential source of charitable income. This is particularly so if the category is extended to include prospective or potential patients, which for an acute general hospital will include virtually everyone within the hospital's catchment area. The value of this resource in financial terms clearly varies considerably from one part of the country to the next, according to the wealth of the area.

- Large donations from charitable foundations, major corporate donors and wealthy individuals are strongly attracted to the large teaching hospitals, other 'centres of excellence', and other hospitals with a long history or otherwise developed public profile. Such hospitals are overwhelmingly concentrated in London and a small number of other regional centres – as of course are the big donors.

- It is very much easier to raise money for some clinical services or specialties than for others. Paediatrics has the greatest emotional appeal and consequently the highest fundraising profile, but diagnostics and clinical oncology (cancer research and treatment) also have a long-established fundraising capacity. The two largest successful healthcare appeals since the establishment of the NHS were for a children's hospital (Great Ormond Street) and for a hospital specialising in the treatment of cancer (the Royal Marsden). In comparison, the fundraising capacity of geriatrics, mental healthcare and the other Cinderella services is tiny.

- The single area of healthcare that benefits most from charitable status is, paradoxically, private medicine. Thirty seven per cent of private acute hospitals are charities, even though their primary – in many cases exclusive – function is to provide healthcare to private patients (see chapter 4).

One final aspect of the problem of equity in relation to charitable healthcare is captured in Nye Bevan's remark that 'The benefactor tends also to become a petty tyrant, not only willing his cash but sending his instructions along with it'. Modern state healthcare as practised by the NHS is based on identifying the pattern and levels of need within a population and then seeking to deploy resources so as to maximise their effect in meeting that need. Charitable donations, by contrast, are typically motivated by emotional reasons, personal or family ties, or geographical proximity – not necessarily irrational motives, but those which are rarely directly related to relative healthcare need.

Bevan, of course, was well-known for his dislike of charity, particularly charity in its more paternalistic manifestations. He was also someone with a solid faith in the virtues of state planning, seeing in it the qualities of efficiency and effectiveness (if not customer service) which are often ascribed to the business sector today. In his speech in the House of Commons introducing the National Health Service Bill in 1946, he reacted to what he saw as the sentimentality of much contemporary opposition to the creation of the NHS, famously remarking: 'I would rather be kept alive in the efficient if cold altruism of a large hospital than expire in a gush of warm sympathy in a small one.'

Although it is difficult not to agree with Bevan's comment literally, many would today take issue with some of the assumptions that underlie his words. In a society where many people can expect to live a third of their lives beyond the age of sixty, and where great advances have been made in the long-term medical management of disease, the notion of health services being based predominantly on 'curing' people, or even just keeping them alive, is seen as problematic. The modern hospice movement, pioneered in the charitable sector, has raised the issue of the quality of death, and focused attention on both the clinical management and the care management of terminal illness.

In fact, as the example of the hospice movement makes clear, many of the qualities which make charitable healthcare so difficult to plan for in a secure and equitable way also make it an invaluable adjunct to a state planned health service. The spontaneity of the voluntary impulse, its ability to draw on high levels of personal or emotional commitment and its 'bottom-up' orientation, all reinforce charity's usefulness in pioneering new services, drawing attention to gaps in existing services and contributing to the development of a more patient-friendly approach.

Bevan's central thesis, however, deserves more serious scrutiny. This was neatly encapsulated in his statement that 'a patchwork quilt of local paternalism is the enemy of intelligent planning'. At what point might the negative aspects of charitable healthcare, as itemised above, outweigh its potentially useful role and the extra money it brings in? And more fundamentally, to what extent are the planning problems associated with charity merely a drawback to its use or, as Bevan hints, actually a threat to the whole enterprise of state healthcare?

Reliance on charity

The insecure nature of charitable income becomes most worrying in one particular scenario: when health services become dependent on it. To what extent, then, has the NHS grown reliant on charity?

We established in chapter 1 that the total amount the NHS received from charity in 1994/95 was between £469 and £553 million. Annual charitable receipts would therefore only be enough to keep the NHS running for some five days a year. On first analysis, dependence on charity seems a long way off.

Chapter 1 also reported, however, that the proportion of current capital investment in the NHS that came from charity was much higher. Of the total value of assets acquired by the NHS in 1992/93, six per cent came from charity, and nearly ten per cent of new equipment was donated by charity. If the NHS as a whole is not relying heavily on charity for the present, it may well become dependent on it for its future.

The story is also markedly different for particular specialties or hospitals. In *Charity and NHS Reform* (DSC 1992), Lattimer and Holly reported how charity, far from being a funder of last resort, had become the first call funder for much diagnostic equipment in the NHS. For example, appeal literature for a scanner fund in Macclesfield explained baldly: 'Most, but not all, scanners in the UK have been bought on the basis of a charitable appeal in the past and to a certain extent this factor has been exploited by the Government and Regional Health Authorities; to go to an appeal is seen as a way of increasing revenue into the NHS.'

Some hospitals have funded generations of diagnostic equipment from charity. Former policeman Mick Lyons launched a £2 million appeal in 1995 to buy and maintain a Magnetic Resonance Imaging (MRI) scanner for Portsmouth hospitals. Ten years earlier, he had been at the head of a successful £1 million appeal to buy a CT scanner, which was named in memory of his mother who had died of cancer. This time the fundraising team hope to raise enough to be able to replace the CT scanner as well, which will soon near the end of its lifespan.

The Macclesfield appeal was started by a terminally ill patient because there was no CT scanner in the district. Patients needing a scan had to go to Manchester, Liverpool or Stoke, accompanied by a paramedic team often with a police escort, an arrangement which was as unhappy for the desperately ill patients as it was an uneconomical drain on the resources of the health authority. Yet despite the fact that CT scans are now considered a necessary and routine diagnostic procedure by most clinicians, many areas of the country still have to rely for their equipment on the motley assortment of patients, publicans and policemen that courageously launch scanner appeals.

Even more alarming is the reliance on charity in the field of neonatal and paediatric care. Baby Life Support Systems (BLISS) is a health charity dedicated to raising money for neonatal life support equipment for NHS hospitals. In a 1993 survey of 207 hospitals in 17 health authorities across the UK, the charity found that hospitals estimated that, on average, 66 per cent of the equipment in their neonatal units was donated by charity. In some regions the dependence on charity was even higher: in Mersey overall up to 90 per cent of equipment was acquired through donation, with around 80 per cent in Wales and the West Midlands. Most extraordinary of all, altogether nine hospitals in the survey were totally dependent on charity for all their equipment (*Survey of Neonatal Resources*, BLISS 1993).

The BLISS survey also punctures a hole in the theory that while NHS managers are happy to exploit the fundraising potential of facilities such as baby units, they make sure that the basic costs of the facility are covered and would move quickly to maintain the service in the event of a failure in fundraising. In fact the survey found that there was a chronic shortfall of equipment in neonatal units, even for the most fundamental items such as intensive care cots or incubators. 'Overall, there was a 16 per cent shortage, but the individual figures were alarmingly high for some of the most essential items: over 25 per cent for intensive care incubators, nearly 30 per cent for blood pressure monitors, and a disturbing 35 per cent for monitors to continuously measure body temperature, the proper maintenance of which is one of the most important factors for survival of premature babies' (BLISS 1993). In addition, much of the existing equipment was reported to be old or out-of-date. Furthermore, staffing levels were seriously short of those specified in guidelines set by the British Association of Perinatal Medicine. Over a third of neonatal units with intensive care cots did not have 24-hour medical cover from a doctor on duty, and although the BAPM guidelines specify that there should be at least one specially-qualified nurse per cot, in some hospitals in Wales, South West Thames and Northern regions there was only one such nurse to every 10 cots.

It is left to the appeal literature to specify the consequences if the donations do not come in: 'Once we had many cots available for sick children with very special and pressing needs and they were not enough... Many [cots] are still idle because we simply cannot afford to run them... Each of these cots could, if in use, help save the lives of more than 40 children each year... We have the skills, the expertise but not the money. To run just one cot for a whole year will drain in excess of £100,000 from our funds and still the clock ticks away as yet another child waits for the care that might save its life' (Guy's Evelina Children's Unit 'Sponsor-a-Cot' Appeal, quoted in Lattimer and Holly, 1992).

About one in ten babies born in England and Wales require special care in a neonatal unit, a total of some 70,000 babies every year. Despite this level of need, it is clear that many hospitals are dependent on charity for the equipment and standard of care they provide in baby units and that if such charity were not forthcoming there would be nothing to replace it. Indeed, neonatal units themselves are unevenly spread across the country and many owe their very existence to charitable donations, most notably the huge benefactions of carpet millionaire Philip Harris.

Despite the fact that as a whole charitable income makes up only a very small proportion of NHS revenue, it is clear then that this has not prevented a significant and potentially dangerous reliance on charity developing in specific areas. The reliance is dangerous because it replaces planned NHS provision with a source of income which is inherently unstable.

Looking at particular services such as diagnostics or neonatal care provides an insight into the financial role of charity and its effect on the planning of NHS services. Charity's role is marginal in the very specific sense that it is often used to meet the marginal costs of services. In all but a handful of exceptional cases, the NHS will supply the clinical infrastructure and meet the overhead costs associated with services, but often in times of financial stringency managers simply do not have the resources to keep services running at their optimum level. It is a situation familiar in the business world and highlights a historic management problem in the NHS, although one that has been exacerbated in some cases by the introduction of internal market contracts following the NHS reforms. In supplying extra income and equipment at the budget margins, charity is nowhere near funding the total cost of most services but it is making all the difference between those services going ahead or not.

Given this situation it is easy to see how dependency develops. Once the marginal or direct costs of a service are largely met by charity, the whole service will crumble once the extra income is taken away. The fundraisers are as painfully aware of this as the hospital managers, which is one reason why there is a constant pressure to raise more and more money each year in the quest for security and the elusive mirage of 'full funding'. It also explains why so many hospital consultants (not, it has to be said, a breed known for their natural humility) are prepared to devote considerable lengths of their valuable time writing begging letters to companies, foundations and wealthy benefactors.

A textbook illustration of how the relationship with charity shifts from opportunity to need to dependency is given by the history of medical research funding. In the post-war years the vast majority of funding for medical research in Britain came from a government body, the Medical Research Council. Although the Council remains the main source of government money for medical research today, the balance as a whole has shifted radically as the medical research charities have become much more important and the Medical Research Council's budget has shrunk in real terms.

The shift was first apparent in the field of cancer research and treatment (oncology), where the charities were traditionally very strong and the NHS correspondingly weak. In an article for the *New Scientist*, medical historian Joan Austoker relates how the charities were anxious to build on the new forms of cancer treatment that had been developed. 'The NHS, however, paid little attention to the need for specially trained oncologists and developed very few oncology centres. Finally, in 1971, the cancer charities intervened. In February of that year the Imperial Cancer Research Fund established a medical oncology unit at St Bartholomew's Hospital in London, which had already been a pioneer in the field. In July, the Cancer Research Campaign and the ICRF jointly set up two clinical professorships to advance studies on cancer. The creation of these chairs enhanced the recognition of medical oncology as a specialty in its own right' (*New Scientist* 15.10.87).

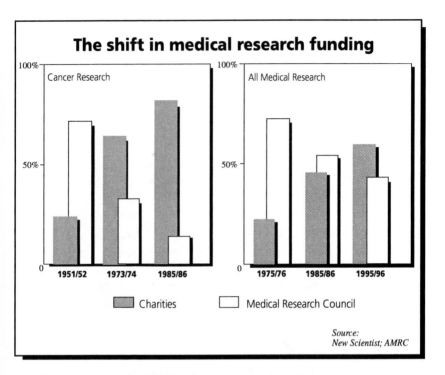

The shift in medical research funding

Cancer Research

All Medical Research

1951/52 1973/74 1985/86

1975/76 1985/86 1995/96

Charities   Medical Research Council

Source:
New Scientist; AMRC

In fact the strength of the cancer charities enabled the Medical Research Council to concentrate its own funds in other fields. Thus whereas in the middle 1970s it was still the dominant presence in medical research funding as a whole, in the field of cancer research it had already been eclipsed by the charities (see figure), a situation which prevails to this day.

Over the last 20 years the shift just described in the funding of cancer research has been replayed over the medical research field as a whole. The charities' overall contribution to medical research crept past that of the Medical Research Council in the late 1980s. By 1995/6 the MRC's budget of £287 million was dwarfed by the combined donations of the research charities (see figure). The bulk of the charities' figure is made up of the £342 million contributed by the 90 member organisations of the Association of Medical Research Charities.

The leverage effect

The factors that make charity an inequitable provider, favouring wealthier areas of the country, were itemised above. But to what

43

extent might this inequity spill over into mainstream NHS services?

Partnership or match funding was one of the political bright ideas of the 1980s. A reluctance to let the state shoulder the full cost of public projects, combined with a desire to give the private sector a greater role, created a new emphasis on funding regimes which brought the public, private and voluntary sectors together. In everything from urban aid to the arts, the aim was to ensure that public grant-in-aid was matched by a contribution from the private sector. Expressed in terminology borrowed from the United States, this led to the phenomenon known as 'leverage', where specific pots of funds or promises of money are used to attract or lever out funds from other sources to make up increasingly complex packages of funding. Project managers or fundraising executives also spoke of a multiplier effect, where the more money you had, the easier it was to attract new money.

In major areas of public expenditure, such as education and health, the contribution of the business sector remained small. One effect of this, however, was bizarrely to increase the leverage power of those contributions that were forthcoming from business and charity, as government sought earnestly to encourage what it hoped would be a growing trend. A prime example of this leverage was provided by the case of the City Technology Colleges, an experiment to bring business into the forefront of educational provision.

The original government scheme was that industry would pay for the bulk of the capital costs of the City Technology Colleges. But suitable private sponsors proved harder to find than expected and the desired contribution from industry was continually revised downwards. The colleges that went ahead, invariably named after their principal private sponsor, in fact typically received less than one fifth of just their start-up costs from non-public sources (the 'private' sponsor was as likely to be an established charitable foundation as a private company or businessperson). There was little doubt, however, that the location of the colleges – dotted around the London suburbs and a few other metropolitan centres – had followed the leverage power of their private sponsors.

In the NHS, the leverage effect attached to large charitable contributions presents a significant challenge to the planning of a service founded on healthcare need. The classic problem inseparable from schemes based on match funding, which could be characterised as 'unto every one that hath shall be given', is clearly also in evidence in the NHS, where the major London teaching hospitals eat up the majority of charitable donations made to the Health Service each year.

Throughout the late 1980s and early 1990s many of the big London hospitals were able to use the money they raised from charitable sources, or their historic charitable endowments, to lever out major capital investment from government. This was despite the fact that ministers had long considered a programme of rationalisation of hospital capacity in London, finally launching the London Review in 1993 after the publication of the Tomlinson report. Yet in the immediately preceding years the government had made a capital investment of £18 million in St Bartholomew's Hospital, matching over £30 million in charitable donations, and had committed some £100 million to the phase three development at Guy's Hospital to match around £40 million from charitable sources. At the time of publication, both these hospital developments are under threat in the London Review. More details on the fate of charitable investments in the London hospitals are given in chapter 7.

The leverage effect is also present in some other major cities or centres of wealth. A major appeal for the development of a new wing at the Royal Hospital for Sick Children in Edinburgh managed to raise £11 million by 1992. Fundraiser James Tysoe told the *Scotsman*: 'People were quite angry fundraising was necessary for a state hospital. They said "We don't like it but we will certainly support it."' Tysoe's persuasive powers, and the £11 million, were enough to secure a promise from the health board to assume responsibility for the wing which includes a 24-bed surgical ward, four operating theatres, an intensive care unit, and 16 parent and child rooms.

Charity has not just been instrumental in encouraging state investment in particular hospitals but also, most famously, in preventing them from being closed down. The story of the Hospital for Sick Children in Great Ormond Street will be familiar to most readers. Faced with closure, the hospital launched a massive, last-ditch appeal to rebuild much of the decayed Great Ormond Street site. Successful beyond the wildest expectations of the governors, the hospital managed to raise £54 million, capitalising on its contacts with wealthy donors and proximity to the City as well as its natural appeal to the general public. The sum was enough to undertake the building work and secure the commitment of the then Department of Health and Social Security to keeping all the hospital's facilities open, albeit with a continuing requirement of £8 million from charitable donations every year.

Rather less well known is the story of the Tadworth Court Children's Hospital in Surrey, which provides care for children with profound disabilities or with long-term or terminal illness. Tadworth Court was originally part of the Great Ormond Street hospital group and, following a protracted period of uncertainty, was itself threatened with closure in 1982. Local people, staff and parents launched a campaign to save the hospital, backed by an appeal. They were joined by a consortium of charities with professional connections to the hospital including MENCAP, the Cystic Fibrosis Research Trust and the Spastics Society (since renamed Scope).

The Spastics Society's director, Tim Yeo (now a Conservative Member of Parliament) proved a well-placed and able negotiator with the DHSS. Behind him there was an increasingly vociferous campaign, backed with a rapidly growing appeal fund. But at a time of extensive local hospital closures the government could not be seen to back down. Finally, in March 1983, the Secretary of State for Social Services announced an extraordinary decision: that he was inviting the consortium to form a charitable trust to take over the management of the hospital, thereby taking it out of the National Health Service.

On the 1st April 1984 the Hospital for Sick Children at Tadworth Court duly left the NHS and came under the management of a new registered charity, the Tadworth Court Trust. At the time, the hospital had 40 places dedicated to the treatment and care of children with cystic fibrosis and those with complex disabilities. Tadworth Court has since grown gradually, establishing a rehabilitation unit for children with acquired brain injuries and a residential school for children with multiple learning disabilities, originally to provide for the pupils of a special school that was forced to close in Croydon. Since leaving the NHS the Tadworth Court Trust has provided care and treatment to over 1,700 children.

Over all this time, the hospital has consistently had to rely on charity. The 1994 annual report of the Tadworth Court Trust explains: 'During the 10 years since 1983 charitable donations of many varieties have contributed £4 million and have (apart from bank borrowings) provided the only money to initiate and support these developments on site and to provide additional facilities and amenities for the children. Without such support and generosity from our donors, not only would there have been no development on site but the Trust would not have survived at all. Until the year just ended there was always an operating deficit which was usually made good by donations.' To set the scene for a new major capital appeal, the Trust has since attempted to focus its public image by changing its name to the Children's Trust Tadworth.

Yet the hospital's largest source of income by far since 1984 has been that old friend of sick children everywhere in Britain: the National Health Service. The actual deal that the charities managed to strike with the DHSS in 1983 included a government grant of nearly £1 million a year. Over time the NHS contribution shifted from the form of grant-in-aid to fees paid under contract for services delivered (and from 1993 the principal responsibility for funding residential and respite care fell onto local authority social service departments, under the community care reforms). But whatever form it takes, the hospital's bread-and-butter funding continues to come from government.

Both the Children's Trust Tadworth and Great Ormond Street Hospital present heart-warming stories of compassion triumphing over bureaucratic calculation. A tale of the people versus the planners in which the people won. Certainly in both cases the determination of local people and patients' families and the generosity of donors enabled first class services to be retained for the benefit of NHS patients. It may seem churlish to raise questions about such an achievement, but would what was possible in Surrey and in WC1 also have been possible in many other places in Britain?

In celebrating a charity success story it is easy to mistake the relative importance of the two main players. Charity's essential role in the rescue of both Tadworth Court and Great Ormond Street was to raise enough money and apply enough pressure to lever out the ongoing financial commitment of the NHS. Put crudely, charity led the way, but it was left to the NHS to foot most of the bill. And that is a form of NHS funding that is only open to those communities or parts of the country that have access to substantial charitable resources.

Planning and control

In the United States, healthcare is equivalent to a stunning 14 per cent of the country's gross national product. Healthcare costs rose at an estimated eight to 10 per cent every year in the early 1990s, far outpacing inflation. Although its coverage is distinctly patchy by North European standards, the subsidised public health system with its Medicare and Medicaid programmes is also placing enormous pressure on the federal budget. Medicare costs alone have risen from $32 billion in 1980, to $98 billion in 1990, to $143 billion in 1994, to $170 billion in 1996, and are forecast to exceed $200 billion by 1998 (*Guardian* 27.1.1996). President Clinton's attempt to keep soaring health costs under control by introducing a national system of health insurance almost broke his presidency. In France, President Chirac's own attempts to control spiralling health costs are looking equally ill-fated, with the healthcare system already set to run a deficit of 30 billion francs in 1996.

Equivalent to just over six per cent of United Kingdom GDP, the cost of healthcare in the UK is not only very small compared to general healthcare costs in the US but is also lower than the health costs of almost every one of our European neighbours. Yet this country alone benefits from a comprehensive healthcare system open to all, free at the point of delivery.

The NHS record on controlling costs is in fact impressive, although rarely reported other than negatively. In a move the US could only watch with envy, central planning control recently enabled the NHS to shift GP prescribing swiftly to the purchase of generic drugs rather than their overpriced, but clinically identical, branded equivalents. NHS guidelines on prescribing similarly have a clout that must amaze the French, who consume on average four times as many pills as the British and six times as many as the Germans.

Chapter 4 also describes how in the US the combination of private health insurance and non-profit or charitable hospitals has led to massive over-investment in some areas, resulting in a situation where a section of the population is unable to afford health cover but still does not qualify for the Medicaid and Medicare programmes. In comparison, the advantages of a national health service are obvious, both in terms of efficient resource allocation and monopsonist power.

The growing role of charity in Britain's healthcare has, however, exposed a set of serious weaknesses in the central planning powers still enjoyed by the NHS.

- Financial stringency has led to some areas of the Health Service growing dangerously reliant on charity for the marginal costs that ultimately dictate whether a service is delivered or not. This is particularly apparent in diagnostics, paediatrics, and oncology.

- Particular hospitals, specialties or areas of the country with access to substantial charitable resources are able to lever out a level of major capital investment or ongoing revenue commitment from the NHS that would be denied to them under standard NHS financing procedures, with serious implications for the Health Service's claim to provide an equitable service based solely on healthcare need.

- The increasing use of charities to supply services under contract to the NHS (see chapter 5) and the growing role of the independent sector as a provider of NHS acute and nursing home care is creating major discrepancies in both the level and quality of services available across the country.

In 1946 Aneurin Bevan was able to tell Parliament: 'Our hospital organisation has grown up with no plan, with no system; it is unevenly distributed over the country'. It is not a charge that could fairly be levelled against the NHS today. But charity has for some years now made a very important contribution to the development of the NHS, a contribution that Bevan was neither willing nor able to foresee. The purely financial input of charity

– although in many ways the least valuable aspect of its contribution – has also attained a significance wholly out of proportion to its size. It will be a key test for the new NHS whether it is able to appreciate the special role of charity without allowing it to disrupt the planning of a service that patients still need to be secure and public opinion still wants to be fair.

SECTION TWO
Charity and private healthcare

CHAPTER 3
THE PRIVATE SECTOR IN THE NHS

'Privatisation' is the most emotive word in the National Health Service. It is a word that has been deployed with increasing frequency since the launch of the NHS reform programme in 1989. It is used by left-wing politicians as a form of accusation, and by the right-wing think-tanks as the ultimate demonstration of their capacity to think the unthinkable. Despite government assurances that the NHS will remain a public service, the media has used the privatisation bogeyword again and again in articles describing the NHS reforms, sometimes unadorned and sometimes with the addition of the adjective 'creeping' – presumably for sinister effect.

The term 'privatisation', however, has long been used in the field of public policy to refer to the transfer of capital and services from public to private ownership, and as such it is a highly misleading word to attach to the NHS reforms, at least without detailed qualification. Many of the innovations in the NHS that both critics and supporters have dubbed 'private' have led in practice to an increased role for charitable or non-profit services. Even the NHS trust structure, decried at the time of its introduction as a preparation for privatisation, clearly owes a much greater debt to the model of the non-profit service sector than it does to the private sector.

Paradoxically then, one of the principal effects of the constant political rhetoric about NHS privatisation has been to obscure the complex but growing role that both charitable and private provision actually do play in the health service of the 1990s.

- Statutory, charitable and private healthcare providers now compete to provide services in the NHS market, if not on a level playing field, at least in the same arena. NHS patients may be treated in a charitable or private hospital, and private patients may be treated in an NHS institution.

- A growing proportion of patients are being treated privately in charitable or private institutions, both removing a potential burden from the NHS, and subtly affecting the 'residual' care the NHS continues to provide.

- In addition to their charitable fund-raising, NHS trust hospitals are now engaged in a widening range of commercial 'income generation' activities, many of them nothing to do with healthcare, in order to boost revenues; and under the private finance initiative hospitals are required to seek private financing for all new major capital schemes.

- High technology diagnostic equipment, gifted to the NHS from charitable donations, may be used by a hospital for private patients in order to raise income.

- Continuing or convalescent care that many, particularly elderly, patients need on leaving hospital is now primarily provided in charitable or private nursing homes. Local authorities are required to spend 85 per cent of the social security element of their purchasing budget for community care in the 'independent' sector, that is, with charitable or private providers.

- 'Private' hospitals, whose primary purpose is to provide healthcare to fee-paying patients, are often registered charities, benefiting from full tax exemption.

This chapter and the one that follows seek to unpick some of these often complex arrangements and to chart their growth. They ask whether we are in some respects moving to the model of healthcare provision prevalent in the United States, and attempt to evaluate whether the advancing role of charitable and private healthcare in the UK works to the benefit, or to the detriment, of a universal public health service.

The key innovation which has opened the doors to greater private and charitable participation in the NHS is the creation of the internal market, with its split between the purchasers and providers of healthcare. The overriding aim of this innovation was to increase competition (and thereby efficiency) among providers and thus to enable health authorities, GP fundholders and other health purchasers to obtain better value for money. By removing any privileged status held by NHS providers and opening up the market to non-NHS providers, an associated aim of the reform programme was clearly to encourage the independent healthcare sector, bringing it into competition with NHS services.

The model for these changes was of course the private sector itself, where such market-mediated relationships are the norm, and in pushing forward the NHS reforms the Department of Health has consistently emphasised the value of following the private sector example. Launching a new award scheme in 1994 to encourage public/private sector partnerships in purchasing (the '4P Awards'), the then health minister Brian Mawhinney said:

'I am convinced that there is a great deal more we can do to draw practical lessons from experience in the private sector. We need a clearer understanding of how to handle new product or service development; to create positive incentives within contracts to reinforce high standards of performance; and to manage risk-sharing between purchasers and providers.

'The private sector has been tackling these questions for a good while longer than we have in the NHS and, while it does not have a monopoly of wisdom in these areas, I want to make sure that we learn from the best.'

It is notable that the three areas of private sector wisdom singled out by the health minister here – new product development, positive incentives and risk-sharing – are remarkably similar to the three qualities on which the voluntary sector customarily prides itself: innovation, motivation and partnership.

But the charitable sector has also been learning from the NHS reforms. In grasping the opportunities presented by the growth in the healthcare market, some charitable bodies have left their competitors in the private sector far behind – even if members of the general public might be slow in recognising them as charities. We focus on this in the next chapter. Below, we consider the extent to which private care and private provision have experienced a resurgence in the NHS, often ushered in by charity.

NHS hospitals, private care

The CAT scanner at the Tameside Hospital in Ashton under Lyne, like many in the NHS, was bought from the proceeds of a charitable appeal. But this appeal was, by any standards, something special. It was initiated by a young cancer sufferer called Mandy Turner who had been put on an NHS waiting list for a diagnostic scan. Determined that other people in her position who could not afford private care should not have to wait for treatment, Mandy launched a £1 million appeal to buy a CAT scanner for the Tameside Hospital. The appeal target was reached in 1990. Nine days later Mandy Turner died, aged 21.

Three years passed. In 1993, Mandy Turner's parents discovered that the CAT scanner bought with the proceeds from their late daughter's appeal was being used in the treatment of private patients. The Manchester Evening News chronicled the local storm that ensued. The newspaper quoted Sandra Turner, Mandy's mother, saying: 'Mandy started the whole thing off simply because she was put on a waiting list and had to go for treatment at Manchester University in excruciating pain. There was no scanner at all for any patients in our area then... I think private patients should pay for their own treatment in their own hospitals. This scanner was bought for poor people like ourselves and I don't think they should be allowed to use it' (*Manchester Evening News* 14.10.1993).

Robert Sheldon, the MP for Ashton who chairs the influential Public Accounts Committee, was quick to recognise how upsetting his constituents would find the situation. 'The money was raised in small amounts from a large number of people, many of whom didn't have much themselves. This will cause offence to those people because the money was not raised to help subsidise private medicine. Mandy didn't put in all that work, when she knew she was dying, to assist private medicine and private patients.'

But had Tameside Hospital done anything reprehensible? In the NHS internal market a hospital trust sells its services to health authorities, GP fundholders – and to private patients. Tameside's acute services manager sensitively confined his comments to stressing that the number of private patients was small and they were treated like any other patient. 'All patients are treated here purely on the basis of clinical need, be they NHS or private. There is no queue-jumping or preferential treatment' (*ibid.*).

In fact, far from behaving unprofessionally, Tameside Hospital had acted in the way that any other NHS trust would, and frequently does. It is standard in the Health Service for trust hospitals to market and use donated equipment just like any other equipment. That includes using such equipment for private patients.

Following up a complaint in his own constituency of Barrow and Furness, John Hutton MP had earlier that year asked the Department of Health in a parliamentary question what guidance it had issued to NHS trusts and district health authorities concerning the use by private patients of equipment purchased by voluntary local subscriptions. The health minister's reply was brief: 'None' (*Hansard* 27.5.1993, col 677).

However, the Department *had* issued guidance on the pricing of donated resources, which did touch on the use of such resources by private patients. In executive letter EL(90) MB/46 the Department informed NHS managers: 'It is unlikely that donations to NHS hospitals are intended to benefit private patients; full cost, including imputed costs of donated resources, should be charged for those patients.' Yet the same letter advised managers to price services to NHS purchasing authorities in the internal market in exactly the same way: '...in arriving at the costs of delivering services costs should be imputed for significant donated resources where it is practicable to do so.' The Department's guidance, therefore, not only confirmed the use of donated resources by private patients, but instructed managers to use the same principles in pricing them for private patients as for NHS patients.

It is doubtful whether donors to Mandy Turner's appeal would have condoned the use of the scanner by private patients or, if they had known about it at the time, whether they would have contributed at all. It is somewhat ironic, then, that the receipt of generous charitable donations by an NHS hospital, enabling it to buy state-of-the-art equipment, can actually make it more attractive to private patients.

Total private patient income to the NHS amounted to £185 million in 1993/94. This figure has risen by some 12 per cent in each of the previous two years, following a massive 30 per cent increase in 1991/2 when NHS trust hospitals were first established. This income is not evenly spread across the NHS. The breakdown of private patient income by hospital is dominated by a small number of acute general and specialist hospitals, mainly in London. Guy's and St Thomas's Hospitals together brought in £11.5 million in private patient revenue in 1992/3, the Royal Marsden earned £8.2 million in the same year, the Royal Free £6.9 million and the Royal Brompton £4.4 million. Hammersmith and Queen Charlotte's Hospital earned £3.7 million in private patient revenue in 1992/3 and Charing Cross Hospital pulled in £3.4 million.

The correlation between hospitals with an outstanding fund-raising record and those with the highest private patient income is startling. Few residents or visitors to London over the last few years will have managed to avoid St Thomas's £5 million 'Tommy' campaign, or Hammersmith's 'Help Hammer Cancer' appeal, or one of the numerous Royal Marsden fund-raising drives. These three hospitals alone, together with Guy's (which merged with St Thomas's in 1993), have managed to raise over £70 million from charity in recent years. The Royal Free Hospital, the Royal Brompton and Charing Cross are also leading fundraisers.

Is this purely coincidental? It seems unlikely. One probable connection is that private patients are drawn to certain hospitals by many of the same factors, outlined in chapter 2, that donors are: a famous name, a high public profile, a reputation as a 'centre of excellence', and proximity to wealth, whether it is in London or another metropolitan centre. But the key determinants in deciding where private patients go for their treatment remain, not surprisingly, quality of service and price, and the contribution of charity can make both of these considerably more attractive.

Guy's Nuffield House is the private patient unit of Guy's Hospital. Originally established in 1935 through the donations of philanthropist Lord Nuffield, Guy's Nuffield House is now managed on behalf of the Hospital by United Medical Enterprises Ltd, one of Britain's leading private healthcare companies. Unlike most other private hospitals or private patient units, Guy's Nuffield House is able to offer its customers most types of surgery including cardiothoracic, vascular, orthopaedic, ENT, gastrointestinal, gynaecological, and plastic surgery, as well as renal transplants. Advertising for the unit explains: 'As part of the Guy's and St Thomas' Trust, Guy's Nuffield House has available to its patients all the specialist facilities of these two major London teaching hospitals and can thus provide the best possible care and medical facilities for its patients.'

For the majority of people in Britain who rely on the NHS for their healthcare there is of course something reassuring about the fact that the clinical facilities and standard of care in NHS hospitals attract private patients who are prepared to pay large sums for the privilege. It is one of the clearest indicators that there does not really exist, as yet, a two-tier health service in this country. It will do nothing, however, to remove the concern about the growing amount of both public and charitable resources that are going into private patient treatment in NHS hospitals.

Claims that the huge growth in private patient treatment in NHS hospitals is being heavily subsidised out of NHS funds are not just forthcoming from the Labour Party and the health unions. The Independent Healthcare Association, the trade body for the private health sector, has consistently maintained that private patient units in the NHS are being cross-subsidised from public funds. The IHA's interest partly stems from its concern over competition between the NHS and independent hospitals over public patients.

The rules governing private treatment in the NHS, enshrined in six principles contained in the NHS Green Book, dictate that private work is permitted when hospitals have excess capacity and provided such work does not prejudice commitments to NHS patients. A 1994 report into the administrative failures in keeping track of patients at Prince Charles Hospital in Merthyr Tydfil, however, did not merit any changes to NHS procedures according to the Department of Health. Independent Healthcare Association chief executive Barry Hassell argued: 'NHS trusts lack the most basic costing systems and if they go for private work, it allows for massive cross-subsidisation'. Lack of transparency and the absence of appropriate audit procedures to ensure public money was not subsidising private treatment pointed to a basic failure in public accountability. 'We know it's happening,' the IHA told the *Health Service Journal*, 'because private patients are being charged less than GP fundholders' (HSJ 26.5.94).

When the Chelsea and Westminster Hospital announced in 1994 proposals to transform part of its new NHS facilities into a 15-bed pay unit, the case drew a spotlight onto the economics of private care in the NHS. The hospital had only just emerged from a long period of controversy over a massive overspend on its own construction, which cost the taxpayer £200 million. Now, critics argued, 28 NHS beds were being converted into 15 private beds, pushing the capital cost of each bed from £300,000 to £575,000. Taken as a proportion of the entire cost of the hospital building, that meant the taxpayer was being asked to meet a bill of £8,625,000 for the capital cost of the private unit. IHA chair John Randle pointed out that there was no chance of the NHS ever recouping sums of that magnitude from the fees from pay-beds. 'They don't cost them properly and our contention is that they often run at a loss. It is using accommodation, staff and facilities which might be available for the NHS. At the same time NHS patients are languishing in Victorian units.'

But perhaps the most extraordinary aspect of the case went unreported in the press. This is that the actual cost of converting the unit for private patient use was met by a £750,000 loan from the charitable trust funds held by the hospital's special trustees. Charitable donations made to the hospital over the years were being used to turn NHS beds into more luxurious private patient facilities. If pay-beds were being reborn in the NHS of the 1990s, then charity was playing the role of midwife.

In a twist of irony, while private beds are being subsidised in the NHS, the government's waiting list initiative has pushed some health authorities into paying extra for NHS patients to be treated in private hospitals. At the start of 1996 the Wiltshire and Bath Health Commission, an NHS purchasing authority, started negotiating with private hospitals in Swindon and Bath to treat patients who had been on waiting lists at the St Margaret Hospital in Swindon for more than nine months, in order that everyone could be treated within the target time of 12 months. The *Independent on Sunday* reported how in many cases the treatment would be carried out by the same consultant as the NHS hospital would have used – but at far greater expense. A spokesperson for St Margaret's said: 'Had the money been available earlier we could have made plans to keep the work in Swindon and we were hoping to do that. It is disappointing that patients will now go to another hospital and be treated by the same surgeon. It is very frustrating' (IoS 28.1.96).

Making patients pay

One of the key principles underpinning the NHS, and its commitment to providing care free at the point of delivery, is the ban on what is known in the Health Service as 'hybridisation' – charging patients for part of the cost of their care. Patients in NHS pay-beds are, in theory at least, charged for the full cost of their treatment including the consultant's fees, but to allow a mixture of NHS and privately paid services would be to invite the establishment of a two-tier or multi-tier Health Service. The comprehensive ambit of the NHS has shrunk slightly over the years to admit a number of specific exceptions to this rule at the fringes of NHS provision, most notably prescription charges, charges for dental care and most optical care outside of hospitals. But for the rest, hybridisation is banned.

In practice, however, pressure on both purchaser and provider budgets can occasionally lead to a situation where NHS patients are effectively denied treatment unless they are prepared to pay or unless charity steps in to provide the shortfall. In a survey of 150 acute hospitals in 1995, the National Asthma Campaign found that 40 per cent were not able to offer a home nebulising service, even though physicians regard it as a necessary element in the treatment of severe asthmatics. Some hospitals understood that GPs would provide nebulisers, but in actual fact patients either had to rely on charity or to foot the £100 bill for a nebuliser themselves. A nebuliser produces a mist of medication which the patient can inhale to prevent an imminent asthma attack or to recover from one. Without a nebuliser at home, patients have to call out an ambulance. The situation is particularly worrying as people in the lowest income groups are twice as likely to be disabled by asthma – precisely the people who can least afford to pay.

Even the 60 per cent of hospitals that were prepared to lend out nebulisers for home use often could not keep up with the demand. One manager told the National Asthma Campaign 'Most of our nebulisers are donated by relatives of people who have died'.

The treatment of those suffering from severe asthma would be universally regarded as a core service the NHS should provide. Some categories of treatment, however, including cosmetic surgery, sex-change treatment, and fertility treatment, are unevenly available across the NHS depending on the relative scarcity of resources and local purchasing practice. Many NHS managers argue that such services do not fall within their duty, enshrined in the NHS Acts, to provide services 'for the diagnosis and treatment of illness'.

Such kinds of treatment do, however, provide NHS trusts with a potentially lucrative opportunity for their income-generating private work. In February 1996 the Chelsea and Westminster Hospital announced that it would offer private IVF (*in vitro* fertilisation) treatment to infertile couples whose health authority refused to pay, at the same price they would have charged the authority. The decision was a highly significant one because it essentially involved using the Health Service to make available private treatment at considerably less than the usual cost to private patients. Yet the arrangement neatly side-stepped the no hybridisation rule because the patient would be charged for all the NHS facilities and time used. The hospital benefited from the extra income and the consultants from getting more patients than they would otherwise have been able to attract, boosting the work of their units. Private hospitals condemned the arrangement as a blatant instance of predatory pricing, using NHS resources to attract patients from the private sector.

From the public point of view, the Chelsea and Westminster arrangement is potentially dangerous because it smudges within an NHS hospital a very important dividing line between public treatment and private treatment. Outside hospital, however, it is fair to say that this line has been gradually eroded for some years now.

The following is from a letter received by a charitable trust in November 1992 from a case manager at Surrey County Council social services: 'I would be grateful if you could consider assisting Mr X with the cost of essential wheelchair repairs. Mr X suffers from multiple sclerosis. He has no movement in his limbs and is completely dependent on others, and on his electric wheelchair which he operates by use of a chin control. He lives with his wife Mrs X who suffers from congenital spastic paraplegia and is also confined to a wheelchair. Mr X's disability benefits are completely taken up by the costs of his care, which is extensive... The larger part of the money for Mr X's wheelchair was raised in the community some four years ago. The cost of the repairs is £1800...'

Responsibility for the provision of suitable aids for disabled people in the community lies clearly with the local authority, not the NHS; hence this letter was sent from the county council. Whether the council should be turning to charity to fund 'essential' wheelchair repairs is another matter, of course.

The community care reforms phased in from April 1991 also moved responsibility for the provision of much long-term care from the NHS to local authorities, opening up at the same time a large grey area over the provision of continuing care for many of those discharged from hospital. While care is provided in a hospital environment, there is little doubt that the NHS will pay; outside the hospital, as the example of home nebulisers illustrates, it is much easier for responsibilities to be fudged.

Clinical advances have meant that patients are discharged from hospital after surgery much more quickly than they used to be. In the case of frail elderly people, however, that can sometimes be too quick, with a disastrous effect on their prognosis. The clinical director of services at Guy's and St Thomas's Hospitals explained to the *Guardian* in November 1994 that the NHS no longer had any incentive to concentrate on rehabilitation and ensure full recovery before discharging patients: 'When the Health Service was providing continuing care beds, it imposed a discipline on us to achieve the maximum rehabilitation possible because we had to pick up the tab if the patient wasn't able to go home. Now we haven't got that discipline it is possible for us not to worry about spending an extra six weeks or so getting this patient better because we haven't got to hold the long-stay bed for them' (*Guardian*, November 1994).

The distribution of institutional responsibilities matters because NHS care is free at the point of delivery to everyone regardless of income while local authority-paid care is means-tested. Over 160,000 people, mostly the single elderly, are thought to have sold their homes in order to pay residential care fees since 1991. The doubling of the capital threshold for eligibility to state aid to £16,000 in the 1995 Budget is unlikely to affect the rate of forced sales as very few homes are valued under this amount.

But the buck does not stop even there. Despite the increase in their care responsibilities, local authorities do not themselves deliver much of the new generation of long-term care provision; this is entrusted to charities and private care homes. The rules governing funds transferred from the Department of Social Security to local authorities under the community care reforms require authorities to spend at least 85 per cent of the money in the independent sector. Over 25,000 places in local authority homes were lost between 1991 and 1995 (partly reflecting the transfer of local authority homes to the voluntary sector). There was a corresponding increase in places provided by the independent sector, which accounted for 77 per cent of all places in residential care in 1995. Of these, 56 per cent were provided by the private sector and 21 per cent by the voluntary or charitable sector (*Residential accommodation statistics 1995*; Department of Health).

Survey research undertaken for this book (see chapter 5) indicates that one of the key incentives for local authorities to place people in voluntary sector homes is that the cost of care can be subsidised from fundraising. This has aroused considerable concern not just from the charities but also, not surprisingly, from private providers who object to their rates being undercut by what they see as unfair competition.

As the size of Britain's elderly population increases, and healthcare costs rise inexorably, the future funding of long-term nursing and residential care is perhaps the single biggest crisis currently facing the welfare state. The government has encouraged the growth of private insurance cover for long-term care, but this is really only an option for people who are relatively wealthy. The question for the NHS is whether this model of means-tested, independently-provided care will spread to other areas of welfare state provision such as healthcare. Up to now, public opinion and political will have been strong enough to safeguard the principle of healthcare for all, free at the point of delivery, on which the NHS was founded, and to resist the introduction of means-testing and charging – at least within the hospital gates. Even so, the current situation brings to mind Keith Joseph's oft-repeated observation: 'This is a fine country in which to be acutely ill or injured, but take my advice and do not be old or frail or mentally ill here.'

It is not just a matter of principle. The introduction of even modest charges or a system of means-testing can act as a powerful disincentive for some people in accessing care and effectively exclude many of the poorest and most vulnerable. And charity has proved itself in the past to be a merciful but desperately inadequate source of relief. In 1952, Nye Bevan recorded the reaction of the Health Service pioneers to some of their first clients: 'When the National Health Service started and free artificial limbs were made available, it was a revelation to witness the condition of the old ones left behind. It was a grim reminder of the extent to which the crippled poor had been neglected.' In the first three years of the NHS, 81,000 modern spinal supports were issued, 30,000 artificial legs, 6,000 artificial arms and over 112,000 surgical boots (Aneurin Bevan, *In Place of Fear*, 1952).

The private sector contribution to the NHS

To talk about the private sector in the context of healthcare in Britain will generally prompt thoughts of private hospitals and private medical insurance. Some parts of the private sector, however, also lay claim to supporting the NHS.

The Paycare scheme, operated by the Patients' Aid Association, advertises itself as 'the alternative to private medicine schemes for those who care about the NHS'. It is an insurance scheme which pays tax-free cash benefits to members when they go into hospital or need other medical, optical or dental treatment. Originally founded in the nineteenth century, the scheme is open to both users of private medical treatment and users of the NHS, but is clearly targeted mainly on the latter. Indeed, the scheme is used by the employees of some 23 health authorities. The Patients' Aid Association is a non-profit making body and has an associated charity trust which makes donations to the NHS, for the purchase of hospital equipment, and also to medical or health charities. The Association covenants a tax-free block donation annually to the charity trust, and the resulting donations to the NHS alone since 1964 have long passed the £1 million mark.

The largest health cash benefit scheme is operated by the Hospital Savings Association or HSA, which also provides premium-paying members with cash benefits when they need medical treatment. It too has a linked charity, the HSA Charitable Trust. In 1995 the trust donated £260,000 to a total of 22 health charities, including Help the Hospices, the Stroke Association, the Alzheimer's Disease Society, SENSE for Scotland, the Spinal Injuries Association and the Malcolm Sargent Cancer Fund for Children.

With their roots in the pre-NHS friendly societies and hospital Saturday funds, companies like the Patients' Aid Association and HSA continue to meet a need in the time of the NHS. But whereas in the past they protected people against the cost of future medical treatment, their primary role now is to insure their members against the financial hardship that illness or incapacity can bring. Their popularity with both NHS employers and employees testifies to the fact that this role is seen as not incommensurate with the values of the NHS and complementary to NHS provision.

However, recent advertising for the HSA also clearly recognises a commercial opportunity in the shrinking scope of NHS provision: 'Most of us in this country still rely on the NHS to care for our health by providing a wide range of services – not just hospital services but dental and optical care, physiotherapy, chiropody, maternity and much more besides. Unfortunately, as a result of the financial pressures placed on the NHS we are forced increasingly to pay more and more for these vital health care services. That is why HSA SuperPlan membership is so attractive...' As so often with non-profit services at the fringes of the NHS, what was initially a clear addition to NHS provision slides into becoming a replacement.

While the Patient's Aid Association has been donating money to the NHS for over 30 years, on the whole corporate giving to the NHS is a more recent phenomenon, dating partly from the Health Services Act 1980 which for the first time empowered health authorities to fundraise actively. It is a sign of the times that there is now a 'Ronald MacDonald House' at Guy's Hospital in London and at the Alder Hey Children's Hospital in Liverpool, where parents of children treated at the hospitals can stay.

The encouragement of corporate social responsibility generally was a rising theme in the 1980s. It accorded with government enthusiasm for giving the private sector a role in areas of activity which had previously been the undisturbed domain of the public or voluntary sectors (see chapter 2). For its part, the private sector followed the American example and launched a 'One Per Cent Club' to encourage big companies to donate one per cent of their pre-tax profits to charity. The initiative was quickly renamed the 'Per Cent Club' when few companies displayed any real appetite for meeting the original one per cent target. In fact, despite this and a host of other company giving initiatives, the extent of business giving always remained disappointing. Even now, companies are only responsible for some three per cent of the total income of charities in Britain.

Charities and NHS fundraisers alike have resorted to increasingly inventive ploys to chase the limited corporate donations that are available. The 'Sponsor-a-Cot' schemes at some hospitals have already been noted. The Leicester Royal Infirmary sent an appeal letter to local businesses in December 1994 asking them to sponsor a bed – with 1,029 beds to choose from. Having become an NHS trust the year before, the hospital complained of a desperate shortage of funds. A one-off payment of £4,000 would buy the donor company a plaque bearing its name above the sponsored bed, as well as a free medical examination for a nominated employee. The Royal Hospital for Neurodisability in Putney sent a white feather to 300 businesses in the area, with a list of suggestions for corporate sponsorship or employee fundraising to benefit the hospital. The letter explained how the touch of a feather might help a patient to awake from a coma.

Government interest in the business sector as a partner for the NHS had already shifted in the late 1980s to activities where companies could take part on commercial terms. This first took the form of encouraging 'income generation' activities: where hospitals use their spare capacity, or natural assets such as the captive clientele, to make a bit of money from advertising space, car parks, or leasing shop space. However, commercial participation in the NHS did not reach serious proportions until the launch of the Private Finance Initiative in 1992.

The PFI relaxed strict Treasury controls on the use of private capital across the range of public services, seeking to encourage private investment in public sector capital and infrastructure projects, and concomitant risk-sharing. The PFI's main application has been in transport – from the London Underground to the development of toll roads to the £3 billion financing of the Channel Tunnel rail link – but capital schemes in the fields of social housing, education and the NHS were also ripe for market-testing, ministers believed. When he took over as Chancellor of the Exchequer in 1993, Kenneth Clarke quickly set about boosting the profile of the Private Finance Initiative, proclaiming: 'I believe that this development is potentially as important to Britain in the 1990s as privatisation was in the 1980s'.

By the end of 1994/5, the Department of Health could announce that 40 substantial projects with a total capital cost of over £100 million had been approved in the NHS under the Private Finance Initiative. These ranged from leasing schemes for diagnostic equipment to the provision of waste incineration services. The health minister emphasised that larger projects were at the planning stage, and these have since been joined by others, including one involving the building and running of what would be the first privately-owned NHS hospital, in Scotland. Most PFI projects in the NHS, however, have been basically non-clinical, with the private sector responsible for construction, leasing and support services, rather than the operation of clinical services.

A £25 million scheme at St James's University Hospital in Leeds provides what could be a model for PFI projects in the NHS. The deal essentially consists of the sale of hospital land to a consortium of private companies so they can construct a car park and a medical science park, with the hospital using the proceeds to finance the development of healthcare facilities. In all the scheme incorporates the creation of a paediatric wing, the medical science park, a 750-space car park, a new child and adolescent psychiatric centre, a 90-bed patient hotel, and a private patients unit (the last was archly omitted from the Department of Health press release).

Crucially, the Department of Health has emphasised that private investment under the PFI is additional to existing NHS capital allocations. Yet the precedent set in the social housing sector is for private finance gradually to replace public expenditure. Housing associations are expected to raise private finance on the markets to match in part what they receive in

Housing Association Grant (HAG). But in the four years between 1991/2 and 1995/6, the amount available from HAG dropped by over £1.1 billion, cutting its contribution to the total budget of housing associations from 77 per cent to 58 per cent.

In the space of less than a year in the course of 1993, private finance moved from being classed as 'unconventional' in the NHS, to being encouraged as an option when the PFI reforms were introduced in April, to becoming a 'standard option', to there being a requirement to seek private funding for all large capital developments. By November 1993 junior health minister Tom Sackville was telling NHS managers: 'In other words, don't come to us until you have considered private sector alternatives' (Department of Health, H93/1063).

Private investment, like charity, has in many instances been welcomed by the capital-starved NHS. There has naturally been some public disquiet over the actual apportionment of risk between private contractors and the NHS, and over the fact that increasingly NHS services will be delivered in facilities that are privately owned. But perhaps the greatest concern over the PFI lies in the extent to which it encourages the NHS to become involved in private healthcare and commercial spin-offs and in the fact that capital development in the NHS is increasingly being geared to private sector priorities. The leverage effect, described in chapter 2, is at work again. The £20 million PFI project at the Royal Berkshire Hospital in Reading, for example, includes a private patients' wing, two car parks, shops, offices and a leisure centre.

The Trojan Horse

This chapter has detailed a host of instances where private care or commercial interests have established themselves in the National Health Service. In most cases the development of private sector involvement was closely linked with the role of charity in the NHS. Donated assets may enable hospitals to supply certain services to private patients or to subsidise private fees; charity payments may set a precedent for costs to be met other than through the NHS; and charities providing services may establish a pattern of non-NHS service provision into which the private sector can happily step. Charity, in fact, may yet prove to have been a Trojan Horse: something the NHS, desperate for funds, is all too pleased to welcome, only to find that it has opened its doors to a rather different animal altogether.

Perhaps the most audacious instance of this are the self-governing hospitals or NHS trusts themselves. When the proposals for self-governing hospitals appeared in the 1989 White Paper, *Working for Patients,* the privatisation bogeyword was never far from the lips of Opposition spokespeople or the arguments of newspaper columnists. But the government countered, quite justifiably, that the NHS trust structure had nothing to do with private ownership and nothing to do with private profit-making. It was in fact quite a different mould in which the self-governing hospitals were cast.

The creation of NHS trusts brought three main changes to the management of hospitals or other units in the NHS:

- trust hospitals would be taken out of health authority control and run by their own independent boards of trustees or non-executive directors;

- hospitals would not just be responsible for a budget which they spent, as under the old system, but would also be responsible for raising all their own income (mostly in the internal market) and balancing their books;

- trust hospitals would be semi-autonomous. Although their boards were accountable to the Secretary of State, they were able to own and dispose of assets, set staff pay levels and conditions of service, borrow money, sign contracts and develop their own business plans.

The relative autonomy of NHS trusts had implications for their accountability downwards, as well as upwards to government. Unlike health authorities, which are responsible for ensuring that the range of health needs of a given population are met, NHS trusts were, in theory at least, to enjoy relative freedom in deciding which services to provide and to whom, constrained mainly by the contractual obligations into which they themselves would choose to enter.

To anyone acquainted with the operations of a large modern charity, the resulting picture was very familiar. From the non-executive board of (unelected) trustees, to the fundraising imperative, to the relative lack of public accountability, the key features of an NHS trust closely resembled those of a typical service-providing charity or non-profit organisation.

It is important to note that, unlike their fellow creations in the education sector, the opted-out or grant-maintained schools, NHS trusts are not formally charities. They are not, for example, registered at the Charity Commission. Yet when the reforms were first implemented, many people in the voluntary sector, perhaps recognising one of their own, assumed that an NHS trust was a charity. Ferdinand Mount, a former head of the Number Ten Policy Unit, has frequently spoken of NHS trusts as charities.

Given the key input of American thinkers and techniques to the development of the internal market in the NHS, the influence of the non-profit model is perhaps obvious. In the US healthcare is delivered by either non-profit or private hospitals and clinics, with state health provision largely confined to means-tested programmes which pay for the treatment of the poor and the elderly. But both the non-profit hospitals and the private ones are widely criticised in the US for inflating healthcare costs to a level higher than anywhere else in the world. There is also little real distinction between the private and non-profit hospitals, with the non-profits frequently investing their annual surpluses into private subsidiaries and commercial spin-offs including hotels, laundries, pharmacies, car parks, shops and auto-leasing companies.

Although they too are based on the non-profit model, NHS trusts in the UK enjoy a level of autonomy which is greater in theory than in practice, with the NHS Executive at the Department of Health still maintained extensive scrutiny and control. In many ways this could combine the best of both worlds: matching local flexibility and decentralised management with the planning advantages and security of a national service. The rapid development of the Private Finance Initiative, however, has given rise in the UK to the sort of deals and system of priorities that characterise the non-profit model in the US. Just how ill-suited that model is to the delivery of an efficient and equitable health service is illustrated in the next chapter.

CHAPTER 4

CHARITABLE HOSPITALS, PRIVATE BENEFIT

The Nuffield Hospitals are the largest group of acute hospitals in Britain outside of the National Health Service. Private patients' fees from their 34 hospitals in England and Scotland bring the group an income of over £100 million each year. (In terms of hospitals owned, this makes Nuffield some way bigger than the BUPA group with its 29 acute hospitals.) As concern over waiting lists and rationing in the NHS boosted the market for private healthcare in the 1980s, the Nuffield Hospitals prospered. The group drew a trading surplus of between £7 million and £11 million a year in the early 1990s, enabling it to build up funds of £105 million by the end of 1993. These were used to underwrite a bold acquisition programme: first it acquired a 114-bed private hospital in Bournemouth, followed in late 1994 by the take-over of the Warwickshire Private Hospital and the HRH Princess Christian's Hospital in Windsor. The Nuffield Hospitals are in fact all that the private healthcare sector was supposed to be: high-quality, enterprising, and financially very, very successful.

But the Nuffield Hospitals group is also a charity. Its official name is the Nuffield Nursing Homes Trust, and it was registered as a charity in 1962 with the objects 'to prevent, relieve and cure sickness and ill health of every kind...' And while the BUPA group was liable for some £9 million in corporation tax in 1994 just in respect of the health services it runs, the Nuffield Nursing Homes Trust was liable for none. In fact, like other charities, the trust is not only exempt from paying corporation tax but also pays no capital gains tax and is entitled to the mandatory 80 per cent relief on its business rates.

Many people in the charitable world have never heard of the Nuffield Nursing Homes Trust. Yet its annual income is greater than that of Oxfam or the Save the Children Fund or the Royal

73

National Lifeboat Institution (*Henderson Top 2000 Charities 1995*). Unlike these other charities, which gain most of their income from grants, donations and other voluntary sources, the Nuffield Nursing Homes Trust only receives one third of one per cent of its income from voluntary sources. Virtually all its income comes from fees.

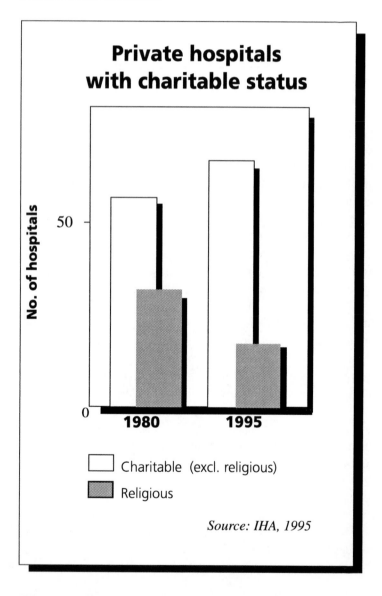

Private hospitals with charitable status

No. of hospitals

Charitable (excl. religious)

Religious

Source: IHA, 1995

However, the Nuffield Nursing Homes Trust is not the only charity which is dedicated to providing health services to private patients. There are now 84 acute hospitals run by charities in the UK, compared with 143 acute hospitals run by conventional private 'for-profit' companies, according to figures published by the Independent Healthcare Association (*Acute Hospitals in the Independent Sector,* 1995). An acute hospital is defined as one which has one or more operating theatres. There are a further 11 psychiatric hospitals with charitable status in the UK.

The 84 acute charitable hospitals in the UK include 17 hospitals which are run by religious charities. The religious hospitals in general have a longer and somewhat different history to the other charitable hospitals, and while the number of other charitable hospitals has risen since 1980, the number of religious hospitals has declined (see figure). Bed numbers tell a similar story. It is notable that the rise in the number of non-religious charitable hospitals was outstripped, however, by the huge increase in the number of for-profit hospitals over the same period, from 65 to 143 (IHA, 1995). But in a 1992 survey of the surgical procedures carried out in independent hospitals, healthcare specialists Laing and Buisson found that the charitable hospitals carried out a higher proportion of surgical procedures classified as 'major' or 'major plus'.

If charitable hospitals and for-profit hospitals are both concerned with providing services to fee-paying patients in a private acute healthcare market worth £2 billion a year, it may well be asked what makes the charitable hospitals different. What is it about them that enables them to benefit from charitable status and the generous tax reliefs that go with it?

The first, perhaps rather obvious, point to make is that in this day and age they have little to do with poverty or lack of financial means. The job of providing health services to the poor or less well off generally is left almost entirely to the National Health Service. The charitable hospitals are more interested in the other end of the patient range.

The main factor that differentiates charitable hospitals from other private care providers is that they do not distribute dividends or profits to shareholders. This does not prevent them from paying handsome salaries to their senior staff and managers but it does mean that any surplus generated at the end of the year is retained and invested back into the hospital's work – back, that is, into providing services to private patients.

The provision of healthcare or, as it is commonly phrased, 'the relief of sickness', is a purpose that is recognised in law as charitable. This means that a non-profit-distributing organisation established for such a purpose will generally be accepted for registration as a charity, notwithstanding the fact that the healthcare that it provides is of a rather restricted kind. The Three Shires Independent Hospital in Northamptonshire is not an untypical case. The Hospital's governing instrument, dating from 1978, records its charitable objects as: '1) the establishment and maintenance of the Northamptonshire Private Hospital as a hospital and nursing home for the diagnosis and treatment of medical, surgical and psychiatric cases; 2) such other purposes connected with the healing of sickness and the relief of suffering as the Governors may from time to time in their absolute discretion determine.'

The 1994 annual report of the Three Shires Independent Hospital describes its inception. 'In 1978, due to a shortage of beds for private hospital treatment [sic], a committee was formed ... and the building of the Three Shires Hospital commenced in 1980. The funds for the project were raised partly by an appeal to industry, the medical and other professions, the residents in the area, and partly through borrowings.' The industrialists and professionals who donated money to the project were not wrong about the demand for private healthcare, as the report goes on to make clear. 'In 1986, due to the Hospital's success, the Northamptonshire Medical Consultancy Unit was built to increase the Hospital's capacity and facilities.'

But the law places one other requirement on charities, in theory at least. This is that they should exist for the public benefit. Organisations which restrict benefit to a very limited group of people or to, say, the members of a club, will generally not be able to register as charities. This is essentially the reason why an organisation like BUPA (which as a provident association does not pay dividends or profits to shareholders) would not be able to register as a charity: it restricts benefit to its members. Charitable hospitals, by contrast, are open to anyone – providing they have the money to pay.

It may seem a fine distinction. But it is a crucial one, because exemption from payment of a multi-million pound tax bill depends on it. A private hospital is able to get charitable status and avoid paying tax on the grounds that it provides healthcare for the benefit of the public.

It is estimated that the total value of these charitable benefits may exceed £35 million a year. If this is added to the value of the tax relief on private medical insurance introduced in 1990 – now worth £85 million annually – the total cost to the taxpayer of subsidising private healthcare comes to over £120 million every year.

From caring for the poor to caring for the well-off

Tracking the history of charitable hospitals since Victorian times demonstrates very clearly how their role in society has changed and in particular how their function of providing benefit to the public has been radically reinterpreted. The Hospital of St John and St Elizabeth in London is a fascinating example.

The hospital was founded in 1856 in the midst of public outrage over the treatment of the wounded following the outbreak of the Crimean war. A testimony to compassion, the new hospital was placed under the charge of four Sisters of Mercy returned from the Crimea, part of the 'Angel Band' as Florence Nightingale and her nurses were called. The work grew over the years, but by the turn of the century the compassion was tempered by financial exigency. A special Charity Commission scheme drawn up in 1898 stated that 'Every donor of not less than £500 as endowment of the Hospital shall be entitled for life to the privilege of always filling one bed in the Hospital'. In 1931 a further scheme empowered the Hospital to take private patients, albeit within strict limits: '...twenty rooms in the Hospital buildings may be appropriated as private rooms for patients paying fees not exceeding 12 guineas a week, and two rooms in the said buildings may be appropriated as private rooms, to be known as Tetley rooms, for patients paying fees of £2.10s a week'.

The Hospital of St John and St Elizabeth was far from unusual in gradually attracting more and more private patients through its doors over the years. In his history of the welfare state,

Nicholas Timmins records how 'In 1891, 88 per cent of the voluntary hospitals' income came from gifts and investments. By 1938, however, only 33 per cent of their revenue came this way, and less in some cases. Payments from patients had risen from 11 per cent to 59 per cent of their income, financed either out of patients' own pockets, by health insurance through, for example, the middle-class British Provident Association, or from factory savings schemes or Saturday Hospital Funds. These last, into which people paid against future treatment, were run by the hospitals themselves' (N Timmins, *The Five Giants*, Fontana 1996).

By 1967, well over a century after the establishment of the Hospital of St John and St Elizabeth (and some two decades after the founding of the NHS), the income the hospital received from private patients, at £121,000 in the year, already dwarfed its voluntary income from donors (£43,000). But probably the greater part of the hospital's activities still consisted of treating ordinary members of the public, thanks in large part to the NHS and the £80,000 annual income received from the health authority, then the North Western Metropolitan Regional Hospital Board. The hospital nevertheless valued its independence, not least for fundraising purposes. Under the bold headline 'Not State Controlled' the hospital's literature declared in 1967: 'The Hospital of St John and St Elizabeth is not State Controlled. The sick poor are treated free of charge in the wards. Those who are able to do so are invited to contribute, but there is, of course, no "means test".'

In 1984 the hospital was still communicating basically the same message, if with a noticeable change in emphasis. The annual report continued to advertise: 'The Hospital is not state-controlled and is therefore dependent on voluntary contributions'. The smaller print went on to say, 'In accordance with the longstanding policy of the Hospital, the private rooms are also available for those patients who can only pay part of the fee – or none. The only considerations being the individual need and the financial resources of the Hospital.' The hospital's financial resources by this time were not inconsiderable. A redevelopment appeal, launched four years previously, had raised over £1 million.

Nowadays the Hospital of St John and St Elizabeth is very largely dedicated to providing private healthcare. The 1993 accounts record that 'the principal activities of the organisation continued to be the provision of private healthcare and St John's Hospice which is funded from the private healthcare activities'. The accounts duly make a distinction between 'private patients services' and 'charitable services'. In 1991, £5.3 million was spent on private patient services, compared to £738,000 on charitable services. Over the following two years, while £3.1 million was spent on charitable services, £12.4 million was spent on private patient services.

Yet the charitable status of the hospital itself meant that neither its private nor its charitable activities were taxed. 'As a charity the Hospital is not liable to taxation on any surplus of income over expenditure.' Thus in 1992-3 an untaxed surplus of £1.1 million was made, bringing the hospital's funds up to nearly £4 million.

The Hospital of St John and St Elizabeth, with its illustrious history, provides perhaps one of the best examples of how the functions of the old charitable hospitals have changed radically, (partly influenced, of course, by the creation of a National Health Service which in one stroke assumed responsibility for the healthcare of the ordinary public). From being an institution dedicated to the care and treatment of the most wretched, the hospital has evolved into a modern non-profit business primarily occupied with providing private healthcare to those who can afford the fees.

In fact, in still retaining a major link to its former function in the form of the charitable hospice it runs, the Hospital of St John and St Elizabeth is perhaps a little untypical of modern charitable hospitals. Compare it with one of the country's most famous private hospitals, the London Clinic.

The 1995 accounts of the London Clinic paint the clear picture of a hospital run to generate a surplus. On a turnover for the year of £27 million, a surplus of £5 million was made (compared to £5.2 million the previous year). The Governors' report records: 'The Company is registered as a charity and its activities have remained those of a private hospital and clinic, with a total of 175 licensed beds of which 37 are for day care treatment and 7 operating theatres. Patient activity was higher than the previous year and was satisfactory. However, due to the pressure in margins exercised by the health insurance companies the net revenue did not grow in line with the increased activity.'

A feature of the London Clinic that makes it rare among charities is that its articles of association enable members of the governing board to be paid. Although the staff of a big charity are nowadays invariably salaried, it is customary for the trustees or members of the governing body to be voluntary, and the Charity Commission is generally reluctant to accept a charity for registration if it has a power to pay the members of its governing body. Yet in 1980 an extraordinary general meeting of the London Clinic passed a resolution raising the sum the Board was entitled to receive by way of remuneration in each year up to £20,000. The practice of paying governors appears to have fizzled out by the early 1990s, however, and the 1995 accounts record that no emoluments were received by the governors, other than medical insurance cover.

Against the £27 million in its private patient business, the London Clinic did spend a certain amount in 1995 on providing free treatment: £2,000. Even this is something of an oddity, outside of the clinic's ordinary activities, as the accounts note. 'During 1992, the 60th anniversary of the London Clinic, the Board initiated an appeal to a broad range of potential donors to establish a fund aimed at providing free treatment to a limited number of patients each year who were permanently resident in London, were uninsured and suffering from conditions which impair lifestyle. It was agreed that the fund would be permanent and that any capital sum raised would be invested with the interest only used for the above purposes together with an equal contribution from the Clinic's funds.' The 1995 accounts duly record that 'during the year £2,000 was used to treat patients'.

With the level of fees normally charged at the London Clinic, £2,000 wouldn't go very far. Fees charged to stay at the clinic as a patient range from £360 to £770 a night, not including medical fees (*Laing's Review of Private Healthcare,* Laing and Buisson, 1995). Such rates make it one of the most expensive private hospitals in the country, and place it out of reach of the vast majority of the population, let alone the less well-off. It is instructive, then, to look at the purposes for which the clinic was established back in the early 1930s, and which still legally govern its activities: 'For any charitable object or purpose, primarily for the erection, building, equipping of operating theatres, hospitals, nursing homes, convalescent homes and medical laboratories. The provision, gratuitously or otherwise, of hospital and clinic services for persons in need thereof.' It is hard now not to read those words 'gratuitously or otherwise' without seeing in them a certain irony.

But it would also be a mistake to regard the London Clinic as exceptional. A detailed analysis of the information provided in *Laing's Review of Private Healthcare*, the bible of the private health industry, reveals that on average the rates charged by charitable hospitals were higher than those charged in BUPA hospitals. Private hospitals do not publish detailed pricing information related to patient volumes, for obvious reasons, but they do give a price range. The mid-point of the range can be taken to compare prices across the sectors. While the average mid-range daily rate charged in a BUPA hospital was £222, the average charge for a charitable hospital was £224 a day, and in the non-religious charitable hospitals was £231 a day. This was so despite the fact that charitable hospitals are heavily subsidised by the taxpayer in the form of the extensive tax reliefs they receive as a result of their charitable status.

Surplus or profit?

An argument often put forward by the defenders of public or charitable services is that such services will always be cheaper overall than those delivered privately because no provision has to be made for shareholders' profit. As we have just seen, this argument does not appear to apply in the case of charitable hospitals. One of the reasons for this may be that, although it is rarely described as profit, such hospitals frequently draw a large trading surplus. What is this surplus spent on?

The 1995 Governors' report of the London Clinic supplies one clear answer. 'In conformity with our charitable status this surplus is applied solely towards modernising, refurbishing and generally improving the hospital. During the past twelve months, a sum of £7,362,000 has been spent.

'This includes £1,286,000 on state-of-the-art medical equipment, the development of an up-to-date day surgery unit, a minimal invasive therapy centre, enlarged progressive care and

the expansion of the medical oncology unit. All in-patient rooms now have their own bathroom, etc., "en-suite".'

The report goes on: 'Work has also begun on enlarging our endoscopy unit to three treatment rooms with COSMOS equipment; developing a modern hospital sterilising and disinfection unit; refurbishing our consulting rooms in 149 Harley Street and a feasibility [*sic*] to enlarge and refurbish our pathology laboratories and radiology department. The cost of this will be over £5,000,000.' Needless to say, a renovation and modernisation programme of this scale and range would be almost unheard of for an NHS hospital nowadays.

At the Nuffield Hospitals group the capital investment programme is no less ambitious, although here the refurbishments and modernisations are eclipsed by the acquisition or constructions of whole new hospitals. The group's 1994 report records: 'The capital expenditure for the year was £24 million. This sum came primarily from the cash generated by our activities and by bank borrowings... The addition of the Warwickshire Private Hospital (now the Warwickshire Nuffield Hospital) in September and the HRH Princess Christian's Hospital, Windsor in November were welcome extensions of our facilities. The Bournemouth Nuffield Hospital which we acquired at the end of 1993 has been suitably modified and is proving very successful in meeting demand in the area.

'The refurbishment and development programme continued during the year with major schemes at Wolverhampton, Birmingham and Brentwood. The construction of the new hospital at Brighton continued to progress with ceremonies having been held to mark the laying of the foundation stone and more recently the topping out of the roof. We anticipate that the eventual redevelopment of our existing Hove facility and the new building in Brighton will provide first-class facilities for healthcare in this important South Coast area.' Subsequently to the time covered in the report, Nuffield Hospitals announced in mid-1995 their plans to build a further new private hospital in Hull.

At first sight this frenetic programme of capital investment by the charitable hospitals appears a little strange as it coincides with a slowdown in the growth of demand for private healthcare. Following a period of rapid growth in the 1980s, the number of private medical insurance subscribers plateaued in the early

1990s. Laing and Buisson also quote an authoritative survey undertaken by Williams and Nicol of the Medical Care Research Unit at the University of Sheffield which confirms Department of Health figures on the low occupancy rate in non-NHS hospitals. 'Overall occupancy of independent hospital beds dropped from 55 per cent in 1986 to 49 per cent in 1992/93. Within this overall decline of 6 percentage points, not-for-profit providers fared relatively poorly... Hospitals run by religious orders had lower occupancy rates – 37 per cent in 1992/93 – than any other ownership category.'

In fact if charitable hospitals make a surplus, investing it back into the business is really the only option they have, other than building up a cash mountain. Under their charitable trusts, many hospitals are constrained from applying their funds to anything other than the provision of healthcare and related activities. This may make it seem all the more surprising that large surpluses are consistently made, rather than the hospitals – which are, after all, charities – structuring their businesses to be able to charge lower prices to customers or even to enable some less well-off patients to benefit from the facilities.

But a close look at the activities of some charitable hospitals suggests that meeting demand, let alone extending benefit, is not the primary motive governing their activities. After detailing its capital investment programme, the Nuffield Hospitals annual report also mentions in passing a rather less lucrative facility: 'The Care of the Elderly Centre in Redhill continued to operate in a difficult market. Demand for the services of the care centre and hence turnover grew somewhat during the year. However, it was not possible to improve margins at all. A fundamental review of the future of this facility is being undertaken.'

In fact, the Nuffield Hospitals' annual reports in the 1980s and 1990s consistently reveal an overriding concern for the level of surplus or profit made by the organisation, a concern which might seem more appropriate to a commercial, 'for-profit' company. The 1987 report, for example, explains that 'We had hoped to achieve a surplus of £5 million plus in line with 1986, but the loss of income from those hospitals which were being refurbished, combined with the higher than expected pay award to nurses, effectively reduced our profits.' 'Every effort will be made in 1988 to achieve a higher surplus' (1987). '...the Board has initiated a programme to improve still further both profitability and the operational efficiency of our hospitals' (1988). The major restructuring of the organisation that followed was apparently undertaken for the principal purpose of improving profit levels, as the Chairman explained in 1992 when he noted that it was 'particularly satisfying to report that the surplus for the year was £9 million, an increase of £1.2 million over 1991. This result reflects great credit on the management at both corporate and hospital level, and justifies the time and effort which has been put in over the post three years in restructuring the organisation.'

Many charitable hospitals continue to structure their activities to generate surpluses which are invested into creating even better services for their exclusive clientele, so naturally enabling them to charge even higher prices. For the paid executives that run such hospitals, generally recruited from the private sector, it is the natural way of doing business. For the same executives, investing for expansion also holds the added attraction of increasing the size of their empires – and the salaries they can command.

Should charitable hospitals retain their tax benefits?

In the United States, the non-profit hospital sector has a turnover estimated at $250 billion. Figures from the American Hospital Association reveal that the assets held by such hospitals have grown tenfold in real terms since the 1950s, totalling some $200 billion in 1992. US newspaper the *Philadelphia Inquirer* estimates that the tax exemptions claimed by these hospitals cost more than $8 billion a year in lost federal and state taxes. But what is potentially more damaging for US society is the effect this has on the healthcare economy as a whole. In their book *Free Ride: the Tax-exempt Economy* (Andrews and McMeel, 1993), Pulitzer Prize-winning reporter Gilbert M Gaul and Neill A Borowski explain: 'Because they pay no taxes, many hospitals have accumulated huge profits and used them to build new hospital wings, to buy expensive equipment, and to diversify into other businesses. That has led to overbuilding and overstaffing of hospitals and has helped push healthcare costs out of sight. On any given night, one-third of all hospital beds in America are empty.'

The chief executives of non-profit hospitals in the US frequently earn more than those of for-profit hospitals, the General Accounting Office of the US Congress found in a 1994 survey. Of the 17 top-paying hospitals, awarding chief executives $350,000 or more in 1991, 14 were non-profits.

The US, of course, has no national health service. While government welfare programmes such as Medicare and Medicaid are designed to cover those who could never afford to pay for their own healthcare, the money from these programmes is actually spent on caring for them in independent hospitals. The spiralling cost of healthcare bills generally in the US now takes up a larger proportion of GNP than in almost any other country in the world (see chapter 2), and is in danger of crippling the US welfare system. At least some of the blame for this situation must rest with the non-profit hospitals. A combination of generous government subsidies and the business practices of the non-profit hospitals has helped create a healthcare system in the US that is characterised by over-investment in expensive facilities and equipment and over-payment of senior staff, pushing healthcare costs artificially high. Far from expanding benefit to more people, the effect of the tax subsidy is thus actually to pull proper healthcare further from the grasp of the ordinary citizen.

In Britain, where we do have a National Health Service, this scenario may still seem a long way off. Government support for the rapid expansion in the private healthcare sector in recent years and the drawing of large surpluses by the charitable hospitals mean that it may not always remain so, however. The value of contracts now placed by the NHS and local authorities with independent hospitals and nursing homes has also shifted the map of healthcare provision significantly. While only 7.6 per cent of healthcare by value is paid for privately in this country, the proportion of healthcare that is now provided by the independent sector is almost 19 per cent, or near one quarter of the value of the care that is provided in NHS institutions (Laing and Buisson, 1995). The inflationary tendency of the private healthcare sector has also been noted by no less astute an economist than Nigel Lawson, who has consistently maintained that tax reliefs for the sector are likely to produce 'not so much a growth in private healthcare, but higher prices' (*The View from Number Eleven*, Bantam, 1992).

It is ironic that the charitable hospitals themselves also recognise the dangers of over-investment – although only when undertaken by their competitors. The Chairman of the Nuffield Hospitals stated in 1984: 'I have frequently drawn attention to the growth of competition in the private health sector and to the dangers associated with the haphazard hospital development which have led to over-provision of facilities in various parts of the United Kingdom. Inevitably, this threatens the viability of the sector... Some degree of commonsense now seems to be prevailing and the rate of new hospital development has slowed down but it remains to be seen whether this will continue.'

Yet, despite that fact that occupancy levels dropped at the Nuffield Hospitals in that year, the Chairman did not seem to think that the common sense he had identified should apply to his own company: '...it is essential to ensure that we have an adequate surplus with which to support our development programme... We hope that the recent increase in fees combined with a thoroughgoing economy programme will enable us to do this.' He duly reports on the progress of ten major development programmes at Nuffield hospitals round the country and on the opening of a new hospital in Lancaster. 'When [the current programme] is finished, we will, over three years, have spent £30 million on improving and extending our existing hospitals.'

The Nuffield Hospitals are, of course, a financial success story. But if in the field of healthcare we are tempted to employ a slighter wider measure of success, it is clear that much of the capital investment undertaken by the independent sector as a whole is inefficient, if not positively wasteful. Occupancy rates in the sector, as has already been noted, are now as low as 49 per cent, and the level of fees charged to patients reflect the cost of those facilities that are not being used. If independent hospitals appear to be slow to recognise innovations in modern healthcare that have led to a huge increase in day surgery and a corresponding decline in the need for in-patient care, that may partly be due to the fact that they have traditionally drawn near 50 per cent of their turnover from room charges.

In crude contrast, the NHS has heavily encouraged the day surgery revolution, even at times laying itself open to the charge of sending patients home when they were still in need of care. Healthcare innovation is also used to justify a 'rationalisation' of beds and the closure of some of London's oldest hospitals. If the NHS was able to invest in improvements a similar proportion of its turnover to that available to the Nuffield Hospitals in the last two years, its capital programme would have come to some £3.7 billion annually. But whereas the number of beds available in private hospitals increased by 73 per cent between 1980 and 1994, according to the Independent Healthcare Association, the total of NHS beds fell by more than a third over the same period.

Perhaps the most breathtaking single instance of over-investment in the private healthcare sector was the short-lived Health Care International Hospital built in the early 1990s in Clydebank in Scotland. Lavishly equipped with 21 operating theatres and a five-star hotel next door, the hospital opened in June 1994, planning to treat over 3,000 private patients a year, mostly high-paying overseas patients. It was set up with £50 million from private investors, a loan of £80 million from a syndicate of banks and, astonishingly, £30 million in government subsidy on account of the 1,800 jobs the hospital was expected to create. The hospital attracted less than 100 patients in the first six weeks and resorted to offering cut-price deals on operations to the NHS. When the receivers moved in five months later, only 50 of the hospital's 260 beds were commissioned and only 20 of those were actually filled.

In addition to its role in artificially inflating healthcare costs, the private healthcare sector has also been accused by the Labour Party in the past of creaming off the most lucrative healthcare business – mainly elective surgical procedures – thereby increasing the unit costs of the full range of acute healthcare supplied by the NHS, including expensive accident and emergency and intensive care services. Individually-paid (rather than insurance-paid) private healthcare is particularly heavily concentrated on the elective surgery that private hospitals can supply at marginal cost. This is to say nothing of the hidden subsidy private hospitals receive from the NHS in the form of investment in the teaching and training of medical staff.

The Labour Party has, however, been curiously silent on the question of stripping charitable hospitals of their tax exemption (in the past a similar restraint was not always shown in the case of charitable private schools). This may be due to the fact that a handful of independent hospitals, such as the Benenden Hospital in Kent and the Manor House Hospital in London, have ties with the wider Labour movement. The *Health Service Journal* reported in 1994 on the work of Manor House and the friendly society that ran it. 'The Industrial Orthopaedic Society, which has the support of the TUC if not the health unions, has some 200,000 members drawn mainly from its historical blue-collar base in heavy industry. For an average of £1.70 a week, members are guaranteed unlimited hospital treatment in a range of specialties. Mike Norris, London regional officer of the Industrial Orthopaedic Society, says: "In the past year or two as the NHS has had more problems we have detected a change in attitude. People are slowly realising the NHS is not going to meet all their needs, particularly in places like London, where there are long waiting lists"' (HSJ, 14.4.94).

The history of private medical insurance is closed tied with the development of non-profit friendly societies or provident associations (BUPA itself is an acronym for British United Provident Association), even if today the bulk of insurance is arranged through company or employer schemes rather than through the unions or voluntary associations. But Left-wing think tank the Fabian Society has recently raised the issue of whether in the right political environment friendly societies can be a vehicle again for enabling a wider proportion of the population to benefit from medical insurance.

As the costs of the welfare state, and the NHS in particular, have risen inexorably, there has been renewed interest across the political spectrum in the idea of using tax benefits to boost the proportion of the population covered by private medical insurance. The idea has some logic, Nigel Lawson's argument notwithstanding. Major insurers, like health authorities, are purchasers of healthcare in whose interest it is to encourage lower costs. Hospitals are providers who benefit when prices are high. In a rational tax system, therefore, there is a strong argument that if private healthcare is to be subsidised – on the grounds that it removes some of the burden of care from the state – it should be linked to private medical insurance which is potentially inclusive of a significant proportion of the population and which plays a role in keeping healthcare costs down, rather than to private hospitals which are exclusive and which push healthcare costs up.

It should not be forgotten, however, that private healthcare in this country is still overwhelmingly the prerogative of the well-off. Detailed figures on private medical insurance cover by socio-economic group were collected in the government's General Household Survey up until 1987, and these revealed that while the proportion of the top two socio-economic groups covered was between 23 and 27 per cent, coverage of the great majority of the middle classes was modest at between three and nine per cent and negligible for everyone else (GHS 1987, Chapter 4).

Private hospitals in this country are subsidised in at least four different ways: their medical staff are largely trained by the NHS; their patients rely on the NHS to provide back up emergency and intensive care facilities; the charitable hospitals are largely exempt from paying business rates in respect of either their offices or medical premises; and the same charitable hospitals pay no tax at all on the large annual surpluses they make. But perhaps most extraordinary of all is the fact that these generous subsidies are channelled not into expanding benefit to more people but into over-investment in beds and facilities that pushes the cost of private – charitable – healthcare out of the reach of the ordinary man or woman in the street. The charitable hospitals' tax exemption acts as a wedge which drives the two tiers of the healthcare system further apart.

Private hospitals may well be a natural feature of the economy in a free society. The time has certainly long gone when there was any real political will in favour of their abolition, and no doubt that is a good thing. But should they continue to be subsidised at the taxpayer's expense?

SECTION THREE

Voluntary providers in the mixed economy of healthcare

CHAPTER 5
CHARITY CONTRACTS WITH THE NHS

by Sari Kovats

The NHS reforms represent the introduction of a 'contract culture' into the voluntary health sector. This follows the growth in the late 1980s of contracting between local authorities and voluntary groups providing social and other services. In the case of health services, the purchasing agency will usually be a health authority or a consortium of health authorities, but may also be a provider, such as an NHS Trust, which is seeking to subcontract services to voluntary organisations. This chapter is specifically concerned with contracts between voluntary groups and such NHS bodies, rather than local authorities, but it should be noted that in some fields, such as community care, there are overlapping statutory responsibilities.

There are several manifestations of contracting (MacFarlane, 1990):

- the replacement of grants by contracts as a form of funding arrangement: contracts correspond to a desire for greater clarity, security and accountability in funding arrangements;

- the contracting out of services non-competitively: contracting out is a response to a desire for a more pluralistic pattern of service provision;

- the contracting out of services competitively: contracting out is a response to a desire to reduce the costs of providing a specified service through competition rather than negotiation.

Voluntary organisations will be involved in all these aspects of contracting and there are fears that this may have adverse effects on their distinctive features, such as campaigning and user-involvement. There are also fears that charitable money will be used to support basic NHS service provision.

The findings in this chapter are based on a postal survey of over 200 charities in England and Wales, supplemented with qualitative information gathered through in-depth interviews with six voluntary organisation directors and four NHS purchasing managers, as well as with the representatives of umbrella voluntary organisations. The research was carried out in late 1993 and 1994.

How far are we into the contract culture?

Over five years since the start of the implementation of the NHS and Community Care Act 1990 it seems that contracting has become an important mechanism for the funding of charities by the NHS but only for those charities which fit into the context of current NHS service provision. However, little comprehensive research has been done on the actual level of contracting to date in England and Wales.

It is important to find out whether contracting is being implemented to replace grant funding of existing services or whether health authority purchasers are using contracts to develop partnerships with charities as new service providers, in what is often described as the mixed economy of health care. The survey of health charities carried out by the Directory of Social Change in 1993/4 found that just under half the services that were being provided under contract were defined by the voluntary providers as new services. The services under contract which were not new services were all previously funded by grants from the purchasing authority.

Several national charities, including MIND and Scope (formerly the Spastics Society), have been notified by their member organisations that switching from grants to contracts has allowed purchasers to decrease the level of funding made available. This is achieved by, for example, keeping the payment the same and specifying a higher level of service (Scope), or by cutting both payment and the service purchased in the expectation that the charity will make up the shortfall to keep the service running as before (MIND).

Our survey found that there was little competitive tendering in 1993 (although the situation may have shifted somewhat by 1995), and this was for services such as drug and alcohol services and mental health residential care. A significant number of contracts (a third for all types of charities, and half for MIND groups) were for the care of persons leaving long-stay NHS hospitals (so-called decanting).

For a new service, there are four basic ways for contract negotiations to begin:

1) the voluntary organisation directly approaches the health authority, or other purchaser;

2) the health authority directly approaches the provider;

3) the health authority invites several organisations to provide the service, by either formal (tendering) or informal competition;

4) the voluntary organisation already providing the service under a grant from the health authority enters discussions with the authority about converting to a contract.

In some cases, charities have been pro-active and approached the health authority because they were aware that the closure of a local hospital presented an opportunity for a contract. Some charitable organisations have actually been set up by the health authority, and before the full implementation of the community care reforms in April 1993 this sometimes involved complicated arms-length arrangements to enable their residents to collect state benefits. In some cases, organisations which were actually part of the NHS have become independent and have then obtained charitable status. This occured, for example, in the case of St James House (see Edwards, 1992) and two hospices.

It was expected that health authorities would contract with those charities with whom they already had good relations, usually through existing grant funding relationships. When health authority purchasers were interviewed, the majority said that they would only contract with charities of which they were already aware. Some health authorities have lists of preferred organisations with whom they will consider contracting.

In some areas, a charity may be wooed by the health authority. For example, East Suffolk MIND was a small charity with no paid staff when it was first approached by the health authority.

The charity then had to make the decision to take on NHS service provision. The organisation is now totally dependent on the health authority for funding, but the director felt that it had evolved with the health authority and had a good informal relationship. The organisation was now by far the main independent provider of mental health services in the area. In effect, it enjoyed a monopoly. In this situation, the health authority – in practice a single purchasing manager – obviously had the will to develop the role of the local voluntary sector.

There is some scope that funding from charitable trusts could be used as seed money to set up joint projects between primary health services and voluntary organisations, with the aim that the family health services authority (or successive primary care purchaser) will later pay for the schemes if they are shown to be successful. This might be particularly appropriate for some outreach services, such as those in ethnic minority communities, where a community-based or collaborative approach is often more effective.

Contract negotiation and terms

Contracts are extremely diverse and it is difficult to generalise about patterns in contracting. Each health authority is left to set up its own policy on contracting with the voluntary sector and whereas some health authorities see it as a priority to develop contracts, in others contracting has not really got off the ground. From in-depth interviews with managers of charities with several contracts a few general points on contracting can be made.

Burden of negotiation. Contract negotiations are often long and protracted affairs. Negotiations can last up to a year and sometimes a service will begin without the contract being signed. The negotiations take up a great deal of time for the person responsible, usually the director of the charity, so that they feel that their job description has changed from manager to financial negotiator. One director of a local MIND group said 'I feel I spend most of my time on [contract] negotiation and I would say 80 per cent of that is concerned with cost'.

The rate of change within the NHS has had a knock-on effect on the contracting process. Many health authorities have undergone major restructuring with mergers and the creation of purchasing consortia covering larger areas. Staff changes have meant that the person with whom the provider had been negotiating had moved on. Such changes have been frustrating and 'very disruptive' for the charities involved.

Sub-contracts. In some areas of provision sub-contracts may become more common. In this case the charity sub-contracts with an NHS major provider, usually an NHS trust, which has a multi-million pound contract with the health authority. For example, in south London some drug and alcohol community services are provided under sub-contract. Sub-contracting has the disadvantage that the main contract has to be negotiated first, and the voluntary provider often finds out about its funding only a few months before the service begins. It is also likely that health authority purchasing managers are focused upon the large contracts with major providers and it not surprising that the much smaller contracts with the independent sector are seen as a low priority.

Type of contract. There are basically two different types of service contract. First, there is the cost-per-case contract in which individual treatment or beds are purchased. This contract requires a great deal of price information, but it is also better from the point of view of the purchaser who is only paying for what is received, although the administrative costs are greater. The individual contract is the suggested mechanism whereby local authority social services departments purchase care for individuals who should be involved in the decision-making process. The second type of contract is a block contract where the purchaser pays for a broadly defined range of services, for example a block of beds in a home. (There is also a third variation, the cost and volume contract, which combines features of both.) Block contracts are better for the provider because income is guaranteed. There is often tension between providers wanting guaranteed money for bed-spaces in the form of a block contract and the health authority wanting money linked to beds, in a cost-per-case agreement. This is really an issue of cost because providers do not want to carry the risk of empty beds (voids) which cost them money. Some providers had specific arrangements relating to voids: for example, the purchaser would pay for them within predetermined limits.

Length of contract. Part of the government message on contracts is that they provide greater security than grant aid. However, the survey conducted by the Directory of Social Change found that the majority of contracts were relatively short-term commitments, approximately one third for one year only, and one third for three years. There is clearly a tension between voluntary organisation respondents who wanted longer agreements for security purposes, and to make planning easier, and purchasers who wanted short-term contracts because of the uncertainty of their own budgets. Like other terms and conditions, health authorities have tried to renegotiate contracts for shorter lengths, and since the reforms were implemented there has been a trend to shorter contracts. Some contracts are negotiated with annual reviews and six month termination clauses. The power to terminate the contract with no fault or even explanation effectively reduces the security of the contract to the length of notice, which can be as little as three months. Edwards (1992) concluded that contracts offered no more security of funding than grants.

Legality. There have been cases of written agreements where the purchaser has added a disclaimer, for example, 'this is not a legally binding contract' (Davies and MacFarlane, 1990; Edwards, 1992). Legally this is very dubious; the specific legal responsibilities of the parties will depend upon the wording of the contract concerned, but in practice disputes are likely to be resolved before they reach court.

Financial issues

Some charity directors have complained that health authority managers were placing too much emphasis on the cost of services. The attitude of the purchasers was described as 'macho' and 'gung-ho'. There were feelings that the sudden introduction of the contract culture was causing the health authority staff to flex their muscles and be overzealous in negotiations. However, those providers who were interviewed did describe the contract negotiations as ultimately reasonable.

A crucial question is whether the contract or agreement covers the full cost of the service. This is not easy to determine. The majority (67 per cent) of respondents in our survey said that the contract payments did not fully cover their revenue costs. Approximately a third of respondents with contracts said they used fundraising income to supplement the contract payments, 30 per cent said they used volunteers and 16 per cent used a grant from a charitable source (see figure). (Note that these figures sum to more than 67 as some charities cited more than one source of supplementary income.) However, some charities have found that it is not cost-effective to fundraise. Health authority purchasers are also strict about the financial viability of the service provider (charities are often perceived as having little financial awareness) and thus would not want services to depend upon an income that is so insecure.

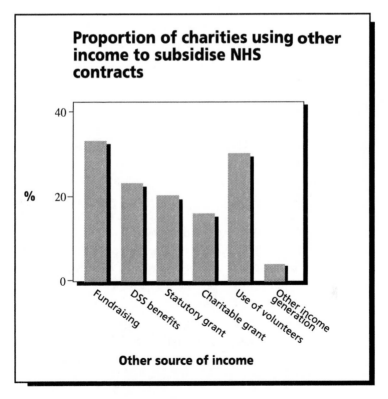

Proportion of charities using other income to subsidise NHS contracts

Other source of income

Revenue costs. Contracts may cover revenue costs (which should be fully costed under the terms of the contract during negotiations) but other factors also need to be taken into account to determine whether the actual level of funding is sufficient. Voluntary organisations need core funding for management costs (sometimes these are included in the contract, sometimes not) and also need to be able to withstand unpredictable factors such as inflation and voids.

There is evidence that health authorities have put pressure on charities to fundraise for certain costs or particular items, and even capital costs such as furnishings. There is a resistance among charity managers, however, to using fundraised income to cover basic revenue costs (Kovats, 1994).

Many residential providers fundraise for parties and outings for the residents, things that are seen as extras. Organisations may also apply to charitable trusts for specific projects, for example to employ temporarily a drama therapist or to publish a local mental health directory. Thus it seems that the voluntary organisations were able to obtain other sources of money to provide innovative services. In addition, some organisations are looking to create posts which are self-financing, for example those of training managers.

Capital costs. Capital costs are defined as the significant costs necessary for starting up a new service. This might include, for example, the costs of buying or leasing and refurbishing the accommodation needed for a residential project. Capital arrangements associated with service contracts for residential care are complex because often the voluntary provider teams up with a housing association. Briefly, there were two main statutory sources of capital uncovered in the survey.

1) The health authority often gave the capital in the form of a loan to a housing association which then had an agreement with the voluntary care provider. The loan was repayable in the case of the project folding.

2) The voluntary care provider and housing association put in a joint bid to the Housing Corporation, which often included a bid for money from the Special Needs Maintenance Allowance (SNMA).

Arrangements were complicated before April 1993 by the fact that in some cases the health authority wanted to distance itself from the capital in order to allow the provider to collect social security benefits on behalf of residents. One of the major reasons given for health authorities' decision to contract with voluntary organisations in the past was that it opened the door to the availabilty of DSS benefits, thereby reducing the cost of the service to the health authority. This factor has been removed following the community care changes introduced in April 1993, however.

Under the NHS internal market there is a system of capital charging whereby statutory providers are required to charge the purchaser a six per cent return on their assets, that is, the value of their land and buildings. One effect of this is to introduce a weighting against the present NHS providers and create a level playing field with new entrants to the healthcare market. However, in the independent sector, voluntary organisations are unlikely to have enough capital to allow them to enter the market unless some help in the form of capital is available. For the organisations which were contacted in this study, the purchasers were willing to provide that capital, although this situation may change with time. Some health authority purchasers which have implemented competitive tendering for residential services have made capital one of the necessary requirements. Furthermore, the heavy start-up costs for new or small organisations may restrict access to the healthcare market to larger, well-established and resourced providers.

Volunteers. Voluntary organisations have the advantage of attracting volunteers. Using unpaid staff to provide services can enable providers to deliver a cheaper service. Many residential services run by charities use volunteers, even live-in full-time ones. In general the attitude among managers interviewed towards fundraising and the use of volunteers can be illustrated by the remark: 'Volunteers only supplement the care. I often describe it by saying we get funding for the cake and the volunteers and fundraising are the icing and the cherry on top of the cake.'

Financial surplus. Another important financial issue for charities operating with contracts is whether or not they are allowed to keep any surplus money under the contract. If a provider finds that after a year there is a surplus left over, in some cases the funder is entitled to take back this money (usually referred to as claw-back) or the provider is allowed to keep the surplus but the amount is deducted from next year's payment. Voluntary organisations should not be making a 'profit' on the service. However, as with all business operations, it is necessary to maintain sufficient cashflow. Two organisations were allowed to keep the surplus from their projects without funding being reduced. This was seen as important for several reasons. First, as a motivation for efficiency. If there was no clear benefit in saving money, that is if the surplus went back to the health authority, it would be harder to encourage staff to be more efficient. Secondly, it increased the autonomy of the organisation, because the provider could decide how the surplus was spent. Another reason was long-term viability. In the first agreement a local MIND group had with the health authority, there was a clause which said that the purchaser would let the provider keep any surplus until it had built up a cashflow reserve, an arrangement the MIND director described as 'more than reasonable'. However the purchaser then wanted to renege on this and the dispute had not been resolved. The director explained: 'We don't have the bricks and mortar aspect that would enable us to go to the bank overdrawn... the only security we can get as an organisation is to gain a substantive sum of money... this is exactly how a commercial company works.'

Bureaucracy. The increase in bureaucracy due to contracts is evident. For example, a typical five-bed residential home for mentally ill people will have a revenue agreement with the health authority, a management agreement with a housing association, tenancy agreements with the residents, employment contracts with staff and, possibly, care contracts with the local authority. In addition, charities have to deal with the relevant statutory regulations, which include those under the registered homes legislation, company law, and the recent Charities Acts, as well as health and safety guidelines.

The contracts also make the charity less flexible. As one director of a local MIND group said: 'When we have just been involved with other providers things can move very quickly. We can locate sources of funding and we can get a project together very quickly. When [services] have to be purchased we have to do the formal process, it gets stuck in bureaucracy and it can take ages... If you want a new worker in this house it has got to go into the budget for next year. You can't have a meeting before April next year.'

Monitoring and quality assurance

An essential part of the contracting process is monitoring the contract. The purchaser has the responsibility to ensure that the voluntary organisation is providing an adequate service. Depending upon the agreement, the charity may be providing an NHS service with all the conditions associated with it. Among the voluntary sector providers who were interviewed there was general agreement that the purchasers were not effectively monitoring the contracts due to lack of time and will.

Although many providers feel that their own internal monitoring is more than adequate there is clearly a risk that sub-standard care may go unnoticed. One director of a mental health charity was being pro-active in developing a new system of quality standards but was becoming frustrated at the lack of interest from the health authority. This lack of monitoring reflects the fact that the focus of the negotiations was often on the financial side of the contract. As one respondent said: 'In negotiations so far we are only speaking to the finance people and not the service provision people.'

In some cases, effective monitoring is only accomplished through the registered home inspectors who visit twice a year. One provider was seriously concerned that lack of monitoring would lead to sub-standard care. In some areas, health authority staff have admitted that monitoring is inadequate. It has also been called a 'grey area' and the use of local authority inspectors has been described as a 'cop-out'. This is likely to remain the case where health authority purchasing directors see their job as focusing largely on financial monitoring and not quality assurance.

The role of voluntary organisations

Historically, voluntary organisations have often been involved in the innovation of new or unpopular services. For example, the voluntary sector was seen as well placed for the provision of HIV/AIDS care because informal or community-based organisations were better able than the statutory sector to manage such issues as sexuality and confidentiality.

However, local relationships may be the most important factor in determining whether and to what extent a health authority supports the voluntary sector in their locality, although this may change as the contracting process develops. There are fears that funding for charities which do not slot into the pattern of local authority or NHS services may be increasingly threatened: for example, small local groups which focus on community development.

Voluntary providers which had originally started as local, community-based organisations acknowledged that contracting had significantly affected their organisations: '[Contracting] has been the final culture shock that has knocked us from being 1970s and early 1980s idealists and wishy-washy *Guardian* readers. I welcome some of the professionalism, I do not welcome running [services] along the policy lines of Fords of Dagenham.' Another charity provider commented: 'Most voluntary organisations have a will to do the best for users and contracts tend to get in the way of this, in the way of their principles.'

However, there is little evidence that such ideals and principles give charities any advantages in the new market. In fact, some health authority purchasers thought charities were distinctly over-rated, possessing little financial acumen, although 'the parents like them'. One director of purchasing said that local charities were 'a mixed bunch, some are extremely good, some expect the health authority to bankroll them because they have little commercial maturity – which filters down to the care.'

Voluntary organisations traditionally have a strong advocacy role on behalf of patients or users of the health services. Many charities have a tradition of active campaigning and there is a wide perception that this is being restricted by contracts. Directors are unable to criticise the health authority publicly for fear of upsetting contract negotiations, 'biting the hand that feeds'. A more practical restriction is that some managers feel they have no time for campaigning because of the contract negotiations.

For locally-organised services, such as those provided by MIND groups, the role of campaigning may be left to the national body which means that local issues might suffer. However, some managers take the view that their campaigning is now done through the contracting process, by influencing the purchasing decisions of the health authority.

Another issue emerging from the contract culture is that of health authorities putting pressure on charities to take on clients with needs they were not created to care for. In many cases, this has involved taking care of people with very high levels of need. For example, a charity originally set up to cater for young people with mental illness who are able to live fairly independently, was being pressured by the health authority to take on geriatric residents who needed nursing home care: 'It is a real problem that one... We have not gone down the registered homes road yet, but we might well.'

It is possible to view contracting as a process of turning charities into quasi-statutory organisations. This is so the more that purchasers try to dictate to voluntary organisations exactly which services to provide. Under some contracts, it may appear that the voluntary organisation is in charge of the referral process, controlling which clients it accepts, but in practice the health authority dictates referrals so that if the voluntary organisation refuses to take a referral the money is reduced accordingly in the following year's budget.

The British Pregnancy Advisory Service now has the majority of its contracts with the NHS for providing terminations. However, this had led to a significant dependency on the NHS. Furthermore, the contracts have led to increased NHS control of the service, such as increased demands for service specifications which have restricted the range of the services provided.

One study also found health authority purchasers making little distinction between private and voluntary residential services, with one respondent pointing out that the main motive of most residential providers, including commercial ones, was to keep 'in business' rather than make lots of money (Kovats, 1994).

User Involvement

Common and Flynn (1994) found that most respondents in their study said that the introduction of contracts did nothing to increase user choice in the service provided. Whether there is a choice of services for purchasers to buy depends upon the availability of providers in the area. Whether there is increased choice for the user will depend upon the purchasing practice of the health authority or local authority. The fact that contracting was causing voluntary organisations to grow in order to achieve economies of scale made them more remote from the user. Therefore users would not necessarily benefit from the plurality of providers.

One of the stated aims of the NHS reforms was to increase user choice in service provision, but many people in the charity sector do not think this has been the case. Charities often have users on their executive committees and therefore can claim to exhibit a higher degree of user involvement than private sector providers. However, the impression amongst providers was that it was the responsibility of the purchaser to ensure that users benefited from the new system: 'In theory the contract benefits the user [more than grant funding], if it is implemented and monitored properly. The fear is that there is not enough expertise and experience [to do this] and it will be detrimental to users.'

Another contract-weary provider commented: 'When the contract people's eyes light up on the number-crunching game, on individual spot contracts, block contracts, whatever it is, the unit costs, comparing unit costs, the competitive tendering, the whole thing, it is detrimental [to the user]. It depends on how well the statutory bodies get themselves sorted.'

As the introduction of contracting out is relatively new, it seems that providers are hoping that the issue of user involvement will be addressed later. However, if there is a trend to more competition between providers and an increase in formal tendering, with its focus on costs, then it is difficult to see how user choice would be increased.

Competition and cooperation

One significant effect of the introduction of contracts on providers was increased competition. There was evidence of both increased competition between providers and the purchaser using the threat of competition to negotiate with providers.

Providers felt that the atmosphere was becoming increasingly competitive amongst voluntary organisations, and voluntary organisations were becoming more secretive regarding negotiations. In addition, they felt that there was covert pressure from the purchasers to reduce costs because of competition from other providers. This often took the form of an 'unspoken message'. For example, purchasers are now demanding annual funding submissions which use the same formula for each provider in order to compare costs. 'Competition will be most clear cut when they say put in your bid for managing [the project's] houses and they invite [...] housing association to put in a bid as well... On occasions they have made rather unhelpful comparisons and they have now accepted that you have to compare like with like.'

Many charities were certainly prepared to welcome competition. 'I think competition's fine. I think we can live with competition, and we do. We need to recognise that competition is not a dirty word. I hear the word "competition" far more than I used to, and I hear the word "cooperation" far less.' One interesting view of the healthcare market was as follows: 'This is a market with two main customers. It is not like the high street with thousands of customers. This is a market with the health authority having a cheque book with over £200 million and a local authority having a cheque book with £5 million in terms of the community care budget transferred from the DSS. What I want to say, to use the analogy of the high street, is that you can either have a high street which consists of the candlestick maker, the baker, the butcher, lots of corner shops, etc., or you can have Sainsbury's, Tesco's, and Marks and Spencer. Now I think you can have competition and choice through either model; it doesn't have to be the soviet single store. You still can have choice with large players.'

However one voluntary organisation has been motivated to seek contracts from purchasers outside the local area because of bad relations with their local health authority. The director did not want the organisation to be financially dependent on this particular purchaser.

In response to this uncertain and evolving market some charities are keen to take on as many contracts as possible. Size is important in placing voluntary providers in a stronger negotiating position. One director felt that 'something was better than nothing'. There does not appear to be a clear strategy in these organisations, which reflects the nature of a market which has no clear ground rules. The manager of a mental health consortium was in the difficult position of competing against organisations which were members of the consortium.

In theory, the NHS market does not contain sufficient numbers of purchasers and providers necessary to create enough competition to keep prices down. In practice, competition between organisations is rarely cut-throat.

Another response to the competitive market is cooperation with other voluntary groups in the area, formally or informally. In Suffolk a local forum of providers has been created specifically to discuss the strategy of the health authority: the providers compare contracts with ones from outside the area and have also discussed the idea of a cartel.

One voluntary sector response to contracting is thus solidarity within the sector. Some local organisations have informal or formal discussions to enable them to gain information about the purchaser. The Voluntary Organisations Disability Group, for residential, domiciliary and support care services, was created by several major national voluntary organisations in response to the NHS reforms to ensure good practice, particularly in the case of contracting (VODG, 1993). In one London borough (Southwark), there have also been plans for voluntary organisations to form a cartel.

It is likely that larger, more bureaucratic voluntary organisations will be better able to compete for contracts, and consequently small groups will be squeezed out or even taken over. The voluntary provider in one study (Goulding, 1993) was chosen because it was seen as a professional body with a stronger management structure. Edwards (1992) found that nationally-organised groups had an advantage over purely local projects: for example, the Children's Society's projects received good support from their regional office. It is also possible that voluntary organisations based in local ethnic minority communities may be adversely affected by the growth of contracting. Such groups often work in a holistic way within their own communities and are difficult to slot into a service-level-oriented approach to funding.

Edwards (1992) found that contracting caused organisations to review management structures and organisational practices. In the last 20 years a growing number of voluntary organisations were founded in response to funding changes and these organisations are likely to be less affected by contracts.

Beyond the short term

Many charities currently with contracts think that competitive tendering will increase: 'I do not think that we are going to have a cosy relationship with the health authority forever and a day. I suspect that in a couple of years they will say that [we] have got to reapply for this contract and it will probably go out to tender.' Another respondent's view was that: 'There is always some bugger in the finance department who thinks that they can save money by introducing unit costs or competitive tendering... I think that in the future the health authority will be more market oriented.'

Many health authorities or purchasing agencies are already implementing competitive tendering. The formal criteria specified for bids include experience of service provision and resettlement; integration with other providers and statutory agencies; and financial viability (there is often concern that voluntary organisations are not always financially secure). In one case, the criteria included access to land, or the capital to buy land, which meant that a voluntary provider would need to team up with a housing association to put in a bid, or find the money elsewhere.

In some cases, health authorities have a list of preferred providers. With competitive tendering, the bids reach farther afield. It is possible that competitive tendering will lead to the break down of the local voluntary sector. One charity in south London unsuccessfully bid for a contract which was awarded to a provider from outside the local area. The manager of the charity felt that this was a political decision by the health authority aimed at avoiding dependency on local providers. Furthermore, successful competitive tendering depends upon the existence of competent providers and so purchasing strategies will vary depending on the service; for example, in the field of residential care many providers are often available, private, voluntary and statutory, but more providers would be available in London than in rural areas. Thus competitive tendering is more feasible in London, providing providers are willing to bid for contracts outside their local area. In rural areas it is more likely that a monopolistic arrangement with the purchaser will develop.

Both purchasers and providers have been on the contracting learning curve, and many of the early problems in contracting have been ironed out. However, it seems that there is a general trend for purchasers to become more inflexible and contracts being negotiated now have much less favourable terms for the provider. Health authorities have been known to try and introduce a replacement agreement with much less favourable terms for one which was negotiated soon after the reforms. One charity had negotiated their first contract to last for 15 years with no reviews; the second contract was for 15 years with three-yearly reviews, and the third agreement was for five years with annual reviews.

The findings in this chapter reflect the position on contracting at a crucial stage after the implementation of the NHS reforms, when purchasing strategies are still being developed. It is particularly important to note that while voluntary organisations are getting their heads down trying to work as best they can within the evolving economy of healthcare, they are doing so in the wider context of major changes in statutory responsibilities for health and social care generally.

The future pattern of statutory responsibility for long-term care is of particular concern to agencies such as the Association for Residential Care, which has 150 members, from both the voluntary and private sectors, providing care to over 10,000 people with a learning disability. In the past many people with a learning disability were cared for in long-stay hospitals, but there is now concern over health authorities' commitment to paying for services in the future as the principal responsibility is shifted to local authority social services departments.

Once a health authority has decanted patients, and the long-stay hospital is closed, the health authority is responsible for those patients until they die. But the Association for Residential

Care asks who will be responsible for the next generation of people, whether elderly or with learning disabilities, who need long-term care? The line between healthcare and social care is a fine one, and local authority social services may be asked to shoulder the responsibility for a new generation of clients with few new resources to pay for it. The public policy debate is likely to intensify about who should be responsible in the future for those people who need long-term care: the NHS, local authorities – or the individuals or families themselves.

Notes

Common, R and Flynn, N, 1992, *Contracting for Care*, Joseph Rowntree Foundation, York.

Davies, A and Edwards, K, 1990, *Twelve Charity Contracts,* Directory of Social Change, London.

Edwards, K, 1992, *Contracts in Practice,* NCVO/Directory of Social Change, London.

Kovats, R Sari, 1995, *Charity and NHS Reform: Voluntary sector experiences of contracting and competition,* MSc dissertation, South Bank University, London.

MacFarlane, R, 1990, *The Impact on Management and Organisation,* NCVO Guidance Notes for Voluntary Organisations No.3, NCVO, London.

Goulding, J, 1993, *A Contract State?* Case Study 5, Centre for Voluntary Organisation, LSE, London.

Voluntary Organisations Disability Group, 1993, *Code of Practice for Contracts and Fee Negotiations*, VODG, London. (Enquiries through Scope or the Leonard Cheshire Foundation.)

CHAPTER 6

THE HOSPICE MOVEMENT: A CASE HISTORY OF CHANGE

by Karina Holly
· ·

> *Why should a large and general need be left to the scanty and scandalously choosy efforts of a patchwork of local charities with one hand in the coffers of the NHS and the other in the church bazaar economy?*[1]

The hospice movement is a voluntary sector success story. Well over £100 million is raised each year by the country's 162 voluntary hospices and the major charities Cancer Relief Macmillan Fund, Marie Curie Cancer Care and Help the Hospices. To some its existence is proof of the lack of provision in the NHS, to others it shows what can be achieved through effort and voluntary activity. Either way the hospice movement is undoubtedly an enduring example of how charitable money has played an important role in the nation's healthcare for many years.

From virtually nothing, the hospice movement has grown to encompass many aspects of palliative care provision, including in-patient units, day care centres, home care and hospital support teams. Pioneered by a dedicated band of volunteers and fundraisers the development of the hospice movement is archetypal of past relations between charity and state. Long celebrated for its ability to identify unmet needs in the population and then initiating innovative action to meet them, the voluntary sector (and the donating public) have fully embraced charitable hospices. Almost 10 per cent of the top 500 fundraising charities in the UK are hospices.

A few hospices have received *ad hoc* support from health

authorities for many years, but government formally recognised the strength of the hospice movement in 1990 when charitable hospices received their first government grant of £8 million. This was quickly followed by a public commitment by the then Health Secretary Virginia Bottomley to a 50 per cent government funding target for hospices. However, the money has not quite followed the political rhetoric. The average statutory input is currently 38 per cent, with a national range of between 10 per cent and 70 per cent. This is not expected to rise in the foreseeable future. In addition, the ring-fenced grant for hospices was abolished in 1994, in favour of leaving hospices to raise income from contracts in the NHS internal market. This has contributed to what Jean Gaffin, the director of the National Hospice Council, describes as a 'general anxiety about NHS contributions to hospices'.

The modern hospice movement began in 1967 with the

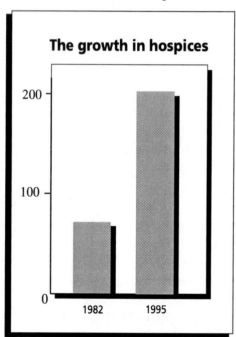

The growth in hospices

200

100

0

1982   1995

founding of St Christopher's Hospice in Sydenham, south London, by Dame Cicely Saunders. The handful of hospices that existed before this date were all run by religious charities. The first of the independent hospices, which were commonly regarded as the anti-institutions of the 1960s and 1970s, St Christopher's was established largely because the institutional care of the terminally ill provided by the NHS was woefully inadequate. The desire for independent status sprung more from a need for a new model of care than any express wish to operate outside the statutory healthcare system. Dame Cicely Saunders vocalised this feeling succinctly, stating: 'We moved out of the NHS in order for principles and practice to move back in'. It was felt that the NHS would only change its own practices towards the terminally ill if a clear model of practice was developed outside the statutory system.

Twenty-eight years on, both principles and practice are now firmly established within the NHS. But although nearly a quarter of hospices in the UK are now NHS units, ownership of the movement is still trenchantly claimed by the independent hospices. The sector continues to mushroom. In July 1982 there were 69 in-patient hospice units. By 1995 this had risen to 208 hospices providing 3,110 beds and charitably-funded hospices account for well over 75 per cent of the hospices and bed spaces available (see figure).

Described by writer and GP Colin Douglas as 'Too good to be true and too small to be useful', the hospice movement is in many ways at a turning point in its development. With the beginning of statutory funding the independent hospices began to move closer to the NHS. By April 1994 the ring-fenced grant was abolished in favour of contracts and many hospices entered the market for the first time. Ironically whilst many hospices have taken on contracts with trepidation, Professor David Clark of the Trent Palliative Care Centre argues that their independent status means they are ideally poised to fulfill many of the market's requirements: 'Here is a real example of the mixed economy of care. Here is a sector where volunteers have played a key role in raising finance (capital and revenue) and in the day-to-day provision of care. Here is a sector where, in some cases, care in the institution and care in the community sit side by side.'

It is also a sector where the distinctions between charitably-funded and NHS-funded hospices are becoming harder to define. Recent research carried out by the Trent Palliative Care Centre estimates that whilst income from NHS contracts and service agreements averages 38 per cent among independent hospices, among NHS hospices it averages 91 per cent of the total (*Health Service Journal* 24.11.95). Each NHS unit is therefore having to raise a significant percentage of its income from charitable sources. The continued strengthening of the purchasers' muscle will pitch NHS hospital against charitable hospice as each enters into contractual relations with the new NHS. The implications all round are significant and as writer Joy Ogden argues, 'Health authorities must learn to become buyers, hospices to become sellers and everyone must learn to become fundraisers' (*Palliative Care* 22.6.94).

Competing with the NHS

A further consequence of the reforms of the NHS is that competition for funds is getting more intense as the shaky barriers between the NHS and charity get further eroded. William Stewart, head of appeals at Manchester's St Ann's Hospice and the chair of the National Association of Hospice Fundraisers, has witnessed at first hand the explosion in hospital fundraising across the whole spectrum of services. Three years ago, St Ann's held regular fundraising functions at nearby Christie Hospital. Now, the Christie Hospital itself employs fourteen full-time fundraisers engaged to raise funds for the hospital and the hospice finds itself in direct competition with what three years ago was its natural supporter base. In addition, Stewart argues, the hospital is able to put on a lavish show because 'at the end of the day they've got resources I can only dream of'.

Pam Rogers, who recently retired as fundraiser at St Columba's Hospice in Edinburgh, has lived with the competition thrown up by NHS fundraising for some years now, working as she did in the shadow of Edinburgh Children's Hospital Sick Kids Appeal. The hugely successful multi-million pound hospital appeal directly hit the hospice's voluntary income, which Pam Rogers estimates fell by about 10 per cent. Even though the hospice anticipated the appeal would affect its income, and attempted to pre-empt it with an increase in advertising, Pam claims they 'felt the appeal's draft'. More recently a fundraising appeal by a Fife-based children's hospice is making things even tighter, but Pam accepts that this kind of competition is now probably here to stay: 'There is now always some major fundraising competition from the NHS, whether it is for a scanner or another piece of equipment or whatever.'

Graham Causey, chief executive at the Princess Alice Hospice in Esher, now expects to compete directly for funds with NHS units. He argues, however, that the playing field is not entirely level, claiming that 'NHS units' real costs are often fudged'. But his greater concern is the lack of strategic planning which has created a situation where NHS units are taking statutory funding away from charitable hospices. Consequently, the Princess Alice Hospice, which currently receives between 23 per cent and 24 per cent in statutory funding, finds itself having to fundraise to meet an annual shortfall.

The view from an NHS palliative care centre, which needs to raise £0.25 million a year, is very different. The palliative care unit at Mount Vernon Hospital in Middlesex opened in 1977 and from the beginning its NHS funding only covered nursing staff. The unit had to find alternative sources of funding to pay for the medical staff and the development of services. The hospital's league of friends has provided the focus to the fundraising and the unit now raises money to pay for day care services, home care services and outpatient care, as well as paying the salaries of two part-time and one full-time social worker.

The Cancer Relief Macmillan Fund is the UK's 13th largest charity, with a total income in 1994 of over £37.5 million, and is a major source of funds for NHS cancer care services. As well as providing pump-priming funding for the eponymous Macmillan Nurses, in hospitals and the community, CRMF also funds GPs, lectureships and oncologists, as well as capital building projects.

In an ironic twist to the NHS versus charity funding debate, the CRMF takes the view that it should concentrate all palliative care funding within NHS units as independent hospices are perceived to be extremely well funded. Paul Rossi, Head of Building Projects at CRMF, also points out that as 80-90 per cent of people who die of cancer never even see a hospice, the NHS has to be the main beneficiary of funds raised.

The Cancer Relief Macmillan Fund is currently raising funds for 40 hospice building projects across the country. Paul Rossi has witnessed the increase in NHS fundraising at first hand, and admits that 'hospitals have begun to fundraise with a vengeance'. However, he is not convinced that this has had a direct impact on local hospice fundraising. If anything, the opposite is often the case: 'When we start an appeal, local hospice fundraising often improves, as we are raising general public awareness about cancer care.' He argues that the real conflict lies not between hospitals and hospices competing for charitable funds, but between old and new styles of fundraising.

At the end of the day, however, the hospice movement's strength is built very firmly on its independence. William Stewart is in no doubt of the priority when it comes to care philosophy or funding: 'If it came to a choice between NHS funding and keeping our independence we would definitely decide to remain independent. The NHS could never provide the same level of palliative care.' Professor David Clark disputes this view stating that 'the [charitable] hospice movement doesn't have a monopoly on attracting volunteers and charitable funds'. With the relationship between the NHS and independent hospices inevitably changing, he sees the future as one of collaboration: 'We are moving into a melting pot of care. Some of the barriers are already beginning to be eroded and some charitable hospices and NHS trusts are starting to collaborate. In the future charitable and NHS providers will have to collaborate to survive.'

Perhaps the contention of Beryl Howard at Mount Vernon Hospital that 'all is fair in love, war and fundraising' will shortly be an axiom embraced by the whole hospice movement, and not just those hospices currently gracing the fundraising league tables.

Notes

Douglas, Colin, 'For All the Saints', *British Medical Journal*, vol 34, 29.2.92

Clark, Professor David, Dr Neil Small and Dr Helen Malson, 'Half full or half empty', *Health Service Journal,* 24.11.95.

Ogden, Joy, 'Voluntary Benefits, Marriage or Merger?', *Palliative Care*, vol 2, no.2, 22.6.94 (published by the *Nursing Times*).

SECTION FOUR
Charitable assets in the NHS

CHAPTER 7

CHARITABLE ASSETS AND THE FUTURE OF LONDON'S HOSPITALS

The National Health Service has become such an enduring feature of British life that it is salutory to remember that there were many moments between 1945 and 1948 when it looked as if it would never happen. The British Medical Association, fiercely defensive of doctors' independence, regarded the NHS proposals with deep suspicion and the health minister, Aneurin Bevan, with something approaching paranoia. At one point a national vote of doctors recorded 86 per cent against accepting service under the new NHS Act.

That the Health Service did not founder completely in its earliest days was due to a number of strategic alliances that Bevan had been able to forge and compromises that he was forced to make. Paramount among the alliances was the understanding he developed with the presidents of the Royal Colleges of Physicians and Surgeons. Looking back in later years on the generous terms he had extended to top hospital doctors to ensure their cooperation with the new National Health Service, Bevan famously commented: 'I stuffed their mouths with gold'.

The comment could equally well have been applied to the great teaching hospitals. Before 1948, hospitals were divided between those under local authority control and those under voluntary control. The 20 teaching hospitals (of which 13 were located in London) were in the latter category, managed by voluntary boards of governors. Financed over the years by public subscription and donations from the wealthy, they had amassed large charitable endowments with which to support their future work. These funds gave them considerable power and independence – and little to gain from a nationalised system of health services.

Bevan knew that the new NHS needed the teaching hospitals,

121

the cream of Britain's medical services, if it was not to be simply the lower tier of a two-tier health system. Without the prestigious teaching hospitals, the Health Service would be condemned to being a poor person's service from the start. His great compromise was this: when the country's hospitals, both municipal and voluntary, came under NHS control, the teaching hospitals were allowed to keep control of their huge charitable endowments.

The bodies of special trustees created to manage those endowments still exist today, the descendants of the old voluntary hospital boards of governors. For many years after the creation of the NHS, the role of the special trustees was largely confined to stewarding the charitable assets with which they were entrusted, ensuring they were wisely invested, and allocating the annual income to research projects, patient welfare and other purposes connected with their hospitals. However, at the start of the 1980s their role expanded to include the revival of active fundraising.

The Health Services Act 1980 provided that health authorities and other NHS bodies 'shall have power to engage in activities intended to stimulate the giving (whether on trust or otherwise) of money or other property to assist the authority in providing or improving any services or facilities or accommodation which is or are to be provided as part of the health service or to assist them in connection with their functions with respect to research'. The dry words of the statute disguised what was in fact a sea-change: for the first time since 1948, the NHS was empowered to spend time and money fundraising from charity.

The 1980 Act provided an indicative list of the activities that were authorised under this new law, including 'public appeals or collections and competitions, entertainments, bazaars, sales of produce or other goods and other similar activities'. This rather quaint list in fact gave little indication of what was to follow.

It started slowly, but by the mid 1980s fundraising had hit big time in the NHS, led by the London hospitals. The names of a number of NHS hospitals, such as the Royal Marsden and the Hospital for Sick Children at Great Ormond Street, have since almost become synonymous with charity. By the end of the decade, in fact, nearly all of London's teaching hospitals had launched major appeals. But many of the hospitals that were benefitting most from this new source of non-statutory income were soon to be those threatened with closure under a sweeping rationalisation of acute health services in the capital.

Donated assets under threat

By the time Sir Bernard Tomlinson published his 1992 report into the future of London's health services, a total of at least £170 million in charitable funds had been invested in the capital development of hospitals in London. A string of further multi-million pound appeals were underway, with a £50 million appeal planned at the Royal Brompton Hospital and another £50 million appeal at St Bartholomew's. Compared with an NHS estate that was still dominated in London by pre-war and Victorian buildings, charity-supported projects like Guy's Hospital Phase III redevelopment presented a model environment for the delivery of modern, high technology healthcare.

The table below lists some of the larger known donations made towards the capital development of hospitals in London in the late 1980s and early 1990s. The list is dominated by the £54 million proceeds of the Wishing Well Appeal to rebuild Great Ormond Street, the £30 million contribution to the redevelopment at Bart's, including a new children's unit and a day surgery unit, the £40 million in donations that went to the Guy's Hospital development, and the £25 million raised by the Royal Marsden that was spent on a new wing at the hospital's Fulham Road site and a new children's unit at its Sutton site. Both Bart's new children's unit and the Royal Marsden's new Fulham Road wing were opened in 1992, in the latter case just weeks before the publication of the report of the London Inquiry chaired by Sir Bernard Tomlinson.

Charitable investment in hospital capital in London

Guy's Hospital	£40,000,000	1989-96
Hospitals for Sick Children (Gt Ormond St)	£54,000,000	1985-92
Middlesex Hospital	£2,900,000	1989-91
National Hospital for Neurology	£10,000,000	1989-96
Royal Brompton Hospital	£2,700,000	1989-91
Royal Marsden Hospital	£25,000,000	1990-96
Royal London Hospital	£600,000	1989-91
St Bartholomew's Hospital	£30,500,000	1986-91
St Thomas's Hospital	£5,600,000	1989-91
University College Hospital	£800,000	1989-91

The recommendations of the Tomlinson report were devastating. London needed better primary and community health services and this called for a 'radical rationalisation' of London's hospitals and medical schools. 'Closures and mergers will be necessary,' the report concluded. 'Proposals in this report, together with changes already planned by the regional health authorities, will reduce the level of productive acute sector capacity by around 2,500 beds.' Tomlinson called for the closure of Bart's and the Middlesex Hospital, the merger of Guy's and St Thomas's, the rehousing of the Royal Marsden and the Royal Brompton in the Charing Cross Hospital building, and the merger of London's nine medical schools into four, as well as a host of other changes.

That many of the hospitals threatened with closure or 'rationalisation' had been the subject of major charitable investment was not entirely lost on Tomlinson. The report noted: 'Many hospitals have been spending heavily on refurbishment and new buildings, some of which developments have been supported by charitable funds. As far as possible, good buildings in strategic locations should be retained in NHS use and poor, ill-sited buildings should be abandoned. However such sunk costs, however recently incurred, are small compared to the revenue costs of the NHS; they should not dictate strategic development in London.'

The idea that health services in London needed a rebalancing of effort between primary and acute care had been proposed on previous occasions before the Tomlinson report, not least in an elegantly argued study by the King's Fund, an influential health think-tank. But that did not dampen the howls of dismay that greeted the Tomlinson proposals, nor pre-empt the campaigns that immediately began to mobilise to save each of the threatened hospitals. To a government already sensitive about its public image on the NHS, it looked as if the political cost of closing some of Britain's most famous hospitals might just be too great.

The charities that had donated money to hospital redevelopments had particular cause to feel outraged. It seemed inconceivable that government had not been aware of the possible outcomes of the Tomlinson inquiry when it was commissioned, yet it had continued to encourage the hospital fundraisers and had stood by while they built and opened their new facilties.

Why had they not been warned? Allowing the new hospital units to be built just in order for them to be 'rationalised' was not just an appalling waste of money. It also seemed an insult to the selfless efforts and generosity of the staff, patients and friends who had painstakingly raised the funds.

A definitive response from the Secretary of State to the Tomlinson proposals was delayed, and delayed again. More studies were announced; task groups were set up. In 1993 Professor Brian Jarman, whose work on deprivation indicators is used throughout the NHS, argued in the *British Medical Journal* that the figures on London's bed capacity used by the Tomlinson inquiry were fundamentally flawed. The King's Fund, too, admitted that their work on health services reorganisation in London had seriously underestimated acute sector need and needed revision. Meanwhile the hospital directors, and the influential special trustees of the hospital endowments, lobbied hard (as of course did the consultants, who in their time had treated more than a few of the inhabitants of Whitehall and Westminster).

At the Department of Health, proposal followed proposal on how exactly London's acute services, and the great hospitals, should be reorganised. The rumour mill ground on. On several occasions particular hospitals appeared to gain a reprieve, only to go back on the danger list again. Other hospitals which had appeared safe under the Tomlinson proposals suddenly fell under threat. It was almost as if Whitehall were deliberately trying to destroy the reputation of the NHS as the last redoubt of effective state central planning.

In February 1994 Health Secretary Virginia Bottomley announced that the Royal Marsden would not be closed and also lifted a threat that had hung over the future of Great Ormond Street. The Royal Marsden had benefited from an intelligent PR campaign, highlighting the quality of the services it offered not just to patients in London but also to the substantial number of referred patients it treated from outside the capital. But perhaps the Marsden's greatest asset was the high public profile and the strings of VIP supporters it had gained through its massive fundraising appeal in the years immediately preceding. Charity came to the rescue at the Marsden, just as it had saved Great Ormond Street from closure ten years before.

125

However, the closure of the main Smithfield site at St Bartholomew's Hospital was confirmed, as was the choice of the St Thomas's site to form the centre of the new Guy's and St Thomas's NHS Trust. At Smithfield, planning immediately began on a radical scheme to save Bart's, with the help of the City, by taking it out of the National Health Service.

Meanwhile, across the Thames at Guy's the donors revolted. The £140 million Phase III building, of which £40 million had come from charity, had been planned as an integrated treatment and research block with wards, operating theatres and high technology intensive care services. The unit was named Philip Harris House after one of the largest donors, a carpet magnate who was a deputy treasurer of the Conservative Party. When it became clear that the unit was no longer planned to house clinical services, the donors started to ask for their money back.

The Philip and Pauline Harris Charitable Trust demanded the return of over £2.5 million it had donated to the unit, and withheld the rest of its proposed £6 million contribution. Lord Philip Harris explained: 'I don't want to drive past Guy's and think: I spent £6 million on that office block when it could have been a hospital' (*Evening Standard* 28.3.94).

Three other charities, the Imperial Cancer Research Fund, the British Kidney Patient Association and the Guy's and St Thomas's Kidney Patient Association, who had committed a total of £3.2 million to the project, similarly requested refunds or withheld their money. The Imperial Cancer Research Fund had invested £1.7 million in Philip Harris House in order to base its breast cancer research programme there, dedicated to developing more effective cancer treatments. Explaining the charity's determination that the project should not fail, clinical research director Professor Nicholas Wright wrote in a letter to the *Guardian:* 'After all, we have a duty to the public – it was their generosity that provided the £1.7 million for Philip Harris House in the first place. We also have a duty to breast cancer patients of the future' (*Guardian* 15.2.94).

A rather different set of priorities had evidently been in Sir Bernard Tomlinson's mind when he noted in his report, 18 months earlier, 'Guy's Phase III building will open in 1994, and will improve the average rating of the building stock, but it is not clear that this will directly enable any significant rationalisation of the estate, or reductions in costs.'

Many of the clinical staff at Guy's, themselves upset at the Secretary of State's decision and how it had been handled, could not help but sympathise with the charities. The chair of Guy's consultants' committee, Dr Bob Knight, commented: 'Philip Harris House was planned over many years. Groups of patients have stood in cold stations with buckets collecting for it. Now they fear for what they have been promised. It will be nothing like they had planned. I can understand their refusal to pay up. It is responsible and sensible' (*Independent* 1.6.94).

Within a month of the decision by charities to ask for their money back at Guy's Hospital, a similar situation was unfolding elsewhere in the capital at another hospital which had suddenly had its future thrown in doubt. At the National Hospital for Neurology and Neurosurgery in Queen's Square a new £30 million wing, the first substantial development of the hospital's building stock for over a century, was under construction. The trustees of the hospital's development foundation announced that they were withholding the final £2 million of their promised £10 million donation towards the new wing, until the future of the site was secured.

Protecting the rights of donors and the public

The scale of the donors' revolt at Guy's was unprecedented. What was more, it was in danger of spreading to other hospitals in London threatened under the reorganisation proposals. The charities certainly had a strong moral argument. Their legal position, however, was more complex.

In most cases of a major capital appeal, the purposes for which money is solicited are given in terms of the named institution to benefit (for example, St Bartholomew's Hospital), the building or facility planned (eg. children's unit) and its primary function (eg. treatment of children with cancer). As we saw in chapter 1, in some cases the appeal will be co-ordinated by the hospital itself and in others by the trustees of the hospital's charitable trust funds. Most of the really major fundraising campaigns, however, will be run by an independent appeal charity, albeit one set up on the hospital's initiative. In each case, the appeal will ask for donations for a specified purpose.

Under trust law, a donation accepted for a particular purpose places on the recipient an obligation to ensure that it is applied for that purpose and no other. There is no necessity for a trust deed, only the existence of a charitable intention. The recipient, in this case either a hospital or a hospital charity, is in the position of trustee for the donated money.

The original purposes of a charitable gift can only be altered if those purposes fail or cannot otherwise be fulfilled (cf. Charities Act 1993, Section 13), in which case the property will normally be applied *cy-pres,* that is, for a purpose as near as possible to the original purpose. An application of property *cy-pres* requires a Charity Commissioners' scheme or an order of court.

One of the central precedents in the development of this branch of law concerns a case from the earliest days of the NHS. In *Re Ulverston and District New Hospitals Building Fund 1956* a public fund had been created for building a hospital at Ulverston but the project was abandoned on the passing of the NHS Act 1946. The court ruled that money donated by known donors should be repaid since it was for a particular purpose which could not be carried out. That part of the fund coming from anonymous donors or fund-raising events had to be applied *cy-pres*. This decision was later embodied in statute (cf. Charities Act 1960, Section 14; now Charities Act 1993, Section 14).

In the case of unspent charitable funds which had been raised by a hospital for a particular purpose, the legal position was thus clear. If the hospital was closed, thereby rendering the purpose impossible to fulfill, Section 14 of the Charities Act 1993 applied and funds had to be returned to known donors with the remainder applied *cy-pres*.

In cases where the charitable money had already been spent, however, legal opinion was divided. The key issue was whether there was any charitable interest remaining and any resulting trustee obligation on the part of the hospital in question. There is a strong argument to say that precipitate closure of a charity-built unit will have prevented the charitable purpose from being fulfilled. The construction of a building, after all, is not in itself charitable: it is its use after construction which enables the charitable purpose to be realised. This would give donors a case for challenging the closure or asking for their money back.

The case is even stronger where charitable funds, once again raised for a specific purpose, have been expended on a unit still under construction. The charitable purpose cannot possibly have been fulfilled here, and the application of the funds on any hospital stock could well be construed in the nature of an investment. There might certainly be a strong claim for charitable interest remaining in the proceeds of any sale of the site.

During the course of 1993 and 1994 the Charity Commission had been seeking extensive legal advice from counsel to try and clarify the situation regarding the future of donated assets to hospitals post-Tomlinson. Finally in July 1994 the Commission issued a statement, based on the legal advice it had received, which was broadly hostile to the notion that donors or charities had any residual interest in donated assets: 'Unless specific terms are agreed... a fundraising campaign to provide capital equipment or buildings for the health services has fulfilled its charitable purposes once the equipment or buildings have been provided and the receiving health authority may do what they wish with them.'

However, a more detailed legal briefing provided by the Charity Commission, although ultimately inconclusive, did specify some of the circumstances in which money would have to be returned to the donors. This is worth quoting in full.

'If a gift has been made to an NHS charity on terms which indicate what should happen to it, then the trustees must give effect to those terms. The following two paragraphs indicate, very generally, what happens if a gift is made without such terms.

'If the NHS trust makes some administrative decision which prevents any part of the gift being spent on the purpose for which it was given (or is instructed to make such a decision) the purposes of the gift fail, "initially" and the money is returnable to the donors, if they can be identified, unless they have waived this right. The Charity Commission could make a scheme directing funds to a similar purpose if donors cannot be traced or do not want their money back.

'If the NHS trust, acting in good faith, starts to spend the money on the original charitable purpose and then something unexpected happens to prevent them carrying on with the project it may be decided that the purpose has originally been put into effect but has failed, "subsequently" in relation to the unused part of the gift. This excludes the right of donors to have the unused part of the gift returned and the Charity Commissioners would make a scheme to enable the remaining money to be spent on a similar purpose. The donors have the right to make representations to the Commission during this process.

'The law regarding the discrimination between "initial" and "subsequent" failure of a charitable purpose has not, however, been fully explored. The terms and conditions laid upon the gift may alter the view taken in any particular case.'

In the light of these complexities, the Charity Commission observed: 'Once an appeal has been launched, every case will have to be considered individually in the light of charity law.' The Commission confined its advice for donors to pointing out that prevention was better than cure. 'We recommend that, before arrangements for an appeal are finalised, the fundraisers should discuss with the receiving health service trustees the terms upon which the appeal funds will be transferred... The imposition of conditions upon donations may well serve to calm the fears of donors but there is a risk that, in setting too tight a constraint upon the conditions under which money is handed over, donors may make it difficult for receiving health bodies to accept the gift.' The Commission's advice raised the spectre of charities registering a charge over buildings to which they contributed with the result that the health authority or NHS trust would have to buy them out if it subsequently wanted to sell the building or put it to alternative use.

While the Charity Commission was tussling with the complexities of charity law, the stalemate in London dragged on. A series of proposals had followed each other on the suggested use of the Guy's site, including turning Philip Harris House into a medical education centre with accommodation for students. Then in April 1995, in what was to be her last major act as Health Secretary, Virginia Bottomley finally announced a string of key decisions on the future of hospitals in London.

The Department of Health had gone a long way to appease the angry donors, unveiling a plan that would make 'full use' of Philip Harris House. The Health Secretary revealed: 'Guy's Phase III (Philip Harris House) will be commissioned for services and academic use substantially in line with original plans. Three-quarters of the space will be used as originally intended. The remaining quarter will be developed as a centre of local in-patient and out-patient services and for medical research and education.'

The charities remained unconvinced. The Imperial Cancer Research Fund maintained that it would not hand over the rest of the money it had raised for the building until its unit was safely installed. The Philip and Pauline Harris Charitable Trust pointed out that the new plan still meant that the hospital would lose over 500 beds. The special trustees cautiously sought reassurances about the clinical future of the building. Construction problems, including major cost and time overruns on the project, further compounded the management headache for the new Guy's and St Thomas's NHS Trust. But with the Department of Health desperate to keep the charities onside and smother the controversy, it looked for the first time as if a compromise were possible.

The National Hospital for Neurology and Neurosurgery, its new charity-supported wing now complete, was told by the Department of Health that it could stay at Queen's Square, although in 1996, with five other hospitals, it came within the management umbrella of the University College London Hospitals NHS Trust. The key role of charity continued. A new £25 million functional brain imaging laboratory, funded by the Wellcome Trust, was officially opened in April at the National, consolidating its position as a world leader in neuroscience. The National's development foundation is currently running a £5 million appeal to create a neuro-rehabilitation facility inside the hospital.

At Guy's, nobody calls the Phase III building Philip Harris House any longer. The remaining millions from Sir Philip (now Lord) Harris never arrived. But the Guy's and St Thomas's NHS Trust did agree an intended use for the block that was close to the original plan. Crucially, the acute services were to stay, although now concentrated on ambulatory or day care. The Guy's special trustees agreed to drip-feed the remaining instalments of their £24 million commitment to the building as each part of it came into commission. The Imperial Cancer Research Fund unit is due to move in during 1997, as are the patients. Whatever it ended up being named, Guy's Phase III had been saved as a hospital.

The combination of moral and technical argument, and public pressure, appeared to have prevailed. Despite Tomlinson's admonition, charity had once again been able to influence the strategic development of health services in London.

The future of the great hospital endowments

While media attention concentrated on the future of donated assets in London, discreet silence surrounded what was potentially an even bigger issue thrown up by the hospital reorganisation programme: what would happen to the charitable endowments of hospitals that were closed?

Of the major hospitals that were identified for closure or merger in the Tomlinson report and subsequent proposals, some were London's oldest. Incredible though it may seem, the history of hospitals such as St Bartholomew's and St Thomas's goes back the best part of a millennium. Their venerable past was perhaps an indication that opposition to their closure would prove fierce. It also goes some way to explaining their wealth.

The charitable endowments that the teaching hospitals had been allowed to retain on the establishment of the NHS had been accumulated over the centuries, typically from the gifts of wealthy donors anxious to buy professionalism and prestige for their hospitals or – as Bevan once hinted – to buy themselves preferment to the House of Lords. But although the endowments stayed put on the passing of the NHS Act, the basis of the hospitals' funding switched from voluntary contributions to state expenditure overnight and public attention went with it. Within the Health Service, the size of the endowments is the stuff of legend; outside it, almost unknown. And Barts, Guy's and St Thomas's are the richest of them all.

Between them they control over £200 million in charitable money. The special trustees who hold the funds are appointed by the Secretary of State and are, significantly, independent of hospital management.

The great majority of the expressed trusts governing the endowed funds are couched in general terms for the benefit of patients in the individual hospitals. Take away those hospitals, and a number of alternatives present themselves. The money could be handed over to the local health authority or to other nearby NHS trusts. There are certainly precedents for the handover of charitable funds between NHS authorities or trustees on previous NHS reorganisations. The funds could remain linked to any residual health services provided by a merged or closed hospital, or the benefit could be inherited by any successor institution. In this case there might be a problem if the functions provided in the new institution did not come within the terms of any of the original trusts. The money, after all, is held in charitable trust for the health of patients and the community, not simply to prop up particular institutions.

There is another option, and one which it was argued would wed Tomlinson's diagnosis of need in the capital with the particular strengths of the voluntary sector. The funds could be joined together to form a new endowed foundation to support the development of primary health care in London. Better general practitioner services, health in the home, in the workplace and in the community: this is where the need is greatest and it is where an independent foundation could take a lead. It could pump-prime technological development in health centres, pilot new models of partnership between the primary and acute sectors in healthcare, pioneer the great shift of out-patient treatments from the hospital to the health centre and the home. As an independent fund such a foundation would also be free – free to innovate and to move quickly to support new ideas, but at the same time big enough to make a real difference.

In 1891, London's parish charities for the poor were amalgamated to form the City Parochial Foundation, now London's largest grant-making charity. A century later, the opportunity arose to profit from that example and to create a new City Health Foundation, to revitalise the capital's primary health services. To date, the foundation has not progressed beyond an idea.

In actual fact, in the case of Guy's and St Thomas's, the merger of the two hospitals has meant that one NHS trust now stands to benefit from a pot of money worth £140 million. This is a unique resource, available to no other hospital in the country. It will also make any objective estimation of Guy's and St Thomas's competitive performance in the NHS internal market very difficult indeed.

For the teaching hospitals in 1948, retaining their endowments was a means of guarding their independence in the face of greater state control. Similarly today, the endowments offer a level of insulation against both market forces and, as we have seen, political decisions. This was clearly perceived by the special trustees at St Thomas's when they spent £160,000 of charitable funds in 1992 on promoting the hospital's image, including a payment of £43,000 to PR agency Lowe Bell Communications.

Fighting for survival after the publication of the Tomlinson report, and haemorrhaging income under the impact of the internal market reforms, St Bartholomew's Hospital struggled desperately in the early to mid 1990s to control its finances and establish its long-term viability. A memorandum to the regional health authority in July 1994 revealed the extent to which the hospital was drawing on charitable money from the special trustees to help balance its books. Commenting on a £5.3 million provision for bad debts in the year, the paper said: 'This provision is a very high one due to the inherent instability of the Bart's financial profile and high level of risk income... A Cost Improvement Programme of nearly £4 million and the receipt of a special trustee grant for £4 million has enabled the unit to establish the bad debt provision at its current level, and still report a surplus for the year.' Examples of grants indicate the extent to which the special trustees bailed out core services in the hospital, including £1.8 million spent on staffing in cardioangiography and radiotherapy services, £400,000 on quality standards in the accident and emergency department, and £600,000 on 'backlog maintenance'.

But it was when all political and legal avenues to prevent the closure of the Smithfield site at Bart's had been blocked, that the role of the Bart's endowment in guaranteeing the future of the hospital began in earnest. An audacious plan was put forward that provided a way of saving the hospital after all – by taking it out of the NHS and turning it into a charitable foundation.

A confidential study commissioned from the King's Fund argued in late 1995 that it made financial sense to keep a hospital at Smithfield, but that it should be run as a charity with a fifth of the site used for private patients with the rest treating NHS patients under contracts in the NHS internal market. The plan was initially given a rough ride by Whitehall officials, anxious that a resurrected Bart's might derail the government's reorganisation programme in London.

But the special trustees at St Bartholomew's and the City of London Corporation, which were jointly funding the feasibility work, secured the agreement of Health Secretary Stephen Dorrell to consider revised proposals in June 1996. Under the proposals the new managing charity, the Bart's Foundation, would include representatives from financial institutions in the City, the City Corporation and clinical staff at the hospital, and would buy the site from the NHS at a heavy discount. The accident and emergency department at Bart's, closed in 1995, would be reopened. 'We are determined that any proposals shall reflect the requirements of both the business and the residential City', a Corporation spokesperson said (*Third Sector* 1.5.96). The City had taken a battering with the renewal of the IRA's bombing campaign and the survival of its hospital seemed central to maintaining its position as the world's leading financial centre. It was certainly an argument that the government would find hard to ignore.

The capital to buy the site would come from charitable funds and from the City Corporation, with ongoing running costs at the hospital funded from a combination of NHS contracts, private patient fees, donations from businesses in the City and charitable reserves. One of the designated members of the new Foundation's governing body enthused: 'This will be an absolute watershed, an alternative way of funding and delivering health care. There is a huge untapped reservoir of charity' (*Sunday Telegraph,* April 1996). It was left to one of the founders of the original Save Bart's campaign, Dr Barbara Bonham-Morgan, to point out that it wasn't actually such a new way of doing things: '[This is] a reason to celebrate the new spirit of hope that Bart's will soon rise again as a charitable foundation, as it was for 850 years before the NHS took it over.'

The proposed Bart's Foundation, in 1996, looks set to take St Bartholomew's Hospital back to where it was in 1948, a voluntary hospital driven by charity and private money. Supporters of the proposal, and the many Londoners who have good reason to love the hospital, would probably commend the foresight of the old hospital governors in extracting that historic compromise from Bevan all those years ago. It would also not be the first facility to have left the NHS and become a charity (see chapter 2). But in talking of the NHS as a mere blip in the 900-year history of their hospital, the Bart's supporters are touching on something momentous.

For London's senior hospital to pass back to voluntary control would send a clear message about the post-reform NHS. Both the international acclaim long enjoyed by Britain's Health Service, and its enduring popularity at home, have depended on something more than its ability to supply healthcare to all, free at the point of delivery. They have also depended on the understanding, shared by health ministers as different as Nye Bevan and Enoch Powell, as well as by hundreds of thousands of doctors, nurses and managers over the years, that the place of prestige and excellence is within the Health Service, not outside it. To that understanding, the loss of St Bartholomew's would be a serious blow.

APPENDIX

How to find out about charitable funds in the NHS

There are over 60,000 individual charitable funds held in the NHS across the country. They are all the result of gifts made by patients, relatives or members of the public that have accumulated over time.

Some of these funds may exist to benefit a particular ward or unit, some to benefit a specific group of patients (such as, for example, children or kidney patients), or they may serve to benefit the work of a hospital generally. The funds may be managed either by health authorities or NHS trusts, or in some cases by special trustees linked to a particular hospital or NHS trust. They are separate from the individual appeal charities often set up to raise money for particular hospitals and from the funds raised by bodies such as leagues of friends.

A charity is a public trust which exists to benefit the community or a section of it. Every member of the public has a statutory right to inspect the records of any charity on the Charity Commission register. These records contain the accounts of the charity, showing how much money it has and what it is spent on; and details of the trusts or the purposes for which the charity was set up and to which all its funds must by law be applied.

However, until the Charities Act 1992 (now consolidated into the Charities Act 1993), NHS charities were excepted from registration with the Charity Commission. The only way of finding out whether there was a fund for a particular NHS unit or group of patients in your area, and how much it was worth, was to ask the relevant health authority or NHS trust. In many cases the authorities – imbued with the culture of secrecy that pervades much of British public life – would simply refuse to provide the information. Sometimes that information, scattered across the authority, would be genuinely difficult to produce.

Health authorities and NHS trusts were required to submit summary accounts covering their charitable funds to the Department of Health but these, when obtainable, did not provide information on individual funds.

Under the Charities Act 1993, NHS charities are now obliged to register with the Charity Commission. The Commission has established an NHS Charity Review unit to identify and register the different funds and bring their regulation in line with that of other charities. The scale of this task, however, means that it is not expected to be complete before 1997. The work is complicated by the massive handover of charitable funds from health authorities to the individual NHS trusts that now manage most hospitals or other NHS services.

Together, NHS charitable funds were worth nearly £1.4 billion in 1995 (see chapter 1). Although they collectively spend some £230 million a year, the amount received every year in donations and other income is generally greater. Despite the levels of financial need in the NHS, a Charity Commission paper noted in 1993: 'It seems that health service bodies tend to accumulate funds rather than to apply them for the purposes for which they were given'. One of the reasons for this appears to be that some NHS bodies assume that the charitable funds they hold constitute 'permanent endowment', that is, funds that they are under a duty to invest, spending only the annual investment return.

In actual fact, only a small proportion of the charitable funds in the NHS comprise permanent endowment and nearly all the money donated to NHS bodies nowadays is obviously given with the intention that it should be spent promptly. Furthermore, the Charity Commissioners have in recent years toughened their stance on unnecessary accumulation of charitable funds: 'Trustees have a duty to apply the income of their trust unless the governing instrument gives them a power to accumulate income or they have a specific application in mind, eg. to provide a building... Even if they have a power to accumulate income that power must be consciously exercised in a proper way with the good of the charity's beneficiaries in mind. A failure to consider the matter and simply allow the income to accumulate without good reason amounts to a breach of trust' (*Charity Commissioners' Annual Report 1992,* HMSO).

From the point of view of the hospitals, however, building up a sizeable charitable fund separate from NHS income can provide a level of future security in what are widely perceived to be troubled times for the NHS. Some hospitals have also been unfairly criticised for not diverting their charitable funds into core running costs or making up budget shortfalls.

In early 1996 the *Sunday Times*, for example, ran an article drawing attention to the fact that Great Ormond Street Hospital had had to turn some children away due to lack of beds and nurses despite the fact that the hospital's special trustees were sitting on £46 million in charitable funds ('Hospital with £46m turns away children', *Sunday Times*, 28.1.96). The trustees pointed out that part of the money was earmarked for specific building or development projects and maintained, quite justifiably, that it would not be appropriate for the money to be spent on core running costs such as nurses' salaries.

The Charity Commission backs this position – up to a point. The Commission has stated: 'It is for ministers to decide the extent to which the state should provide healthcare. The Commission is of the view that it is not a proper use of charitable funds to make provision for which there is a specific statutory entitlement, as in the case of a social security benefit. This does not prevent charities from making provision to supplement that provided by the state.' In practice, of course, the distinction between provision covered by a statutory entitlement and provision that is supplementary has all but collapsed, as dozens of charity appeals for mainstream NHS services now demonstrate.

An individual NHS charity may be governed by a will or a deed of gift or trust which explains what the money is for, or it may simply have its purposes specified in a letter or in a note recording the donor's intentions. Once the NHS Charity Review is complete it is hoped that these details will become easily available to the public through the Charity Commission register, so it will be possible to find out the purposes for which funds were originally donated, as well as the activity on which they are currently being spent.

Of the 60,000 NHS charities that exist, some are clearly very large, but up to half are estimated to have an annual income of less than £1,000. In a few cases, a health authority or NHS trust may hold up to 1,000 charitable funds, so to register them all individually would place a huge administrative burden on the authority. In order to address this problem, a small Act of Parliament was passed in 1995, effectively enabling the Charity Commissioners to give one blanket registration to all the funds held by the same NHS body. The Charities (Amendment) Act 1995 provides that for registration or other purposes the Commissioners may direct that 'two or more charities having the same charity trustees shall be treated as a single charity'.

This will make investigating NHS charitable funds that much easier. An enquirer at the Charity Commission will in theory simply have to give the name of the health authority, NHS trust or (in the case of special trustees) the hospital, in order to find details on all the charitable funds held by that body.

The number and value of charitable funds held by the different health authorities and NHS trusts across the country varies greatly. Although London is particularly well-endowed, many regions elsewhere in the country also have substantial holdings.

NHS charitable funds across England (1992)

	£000
Northern	11,253
Yorkshire	14,476
Trent	24,863
East Anglia	19,713
North West Thames	18,684
North East Thames	14,993
South East Thames	22,641
South West Thames	14,510
Wessex	22,491
Oxford	19,935
South Western	11,043
West Midlands	27,244
Mersey	8,643
North Western	21,495
Special Trustees	371,062
Special Health Authorities	44,334
NHS Trusts (first wave)	41,408

The table gives a breakdown of the amounts held in 1992 before the start of the NHS Charity Review, the last year for which comprehensive figures by region are available (up-to-date figures on total charitable funds held in the NHS are given in chapter 1). The table gives summary figures for the book value of funds held for each of the old NHS regions, for the special trustees, for the special health authorities and for the 57 first wave NHS trusts. These figures are provided to give an indication of the spread of charitable funds across the country, but it should be noted that the funds have considerably increased in size since 1992 and in many cases have also shifted hands: a further 373 NHS trusts have been established since the date of the table. A fully up-to-date breakdown of all charitable funds held in the NHS should be available once the NHS Charity Review is complete in 1997.

Enquiries from the public on individual charities are dealt with by three Charity Commission offices round the country. Broadly, the London office deals with charities in London and the East, the Taunton office with the South and West of England, and the Liverpool office with the North, the Midlands and Wales. The NHS Charity Review section is based in the Liverpool office. The addresses are:

Charity Commission
Graeme House
Derby Square
Liverpool L2 7SB
Tel: 0151-227 3191

Charity Commission
St Alban's House
57-60 Haymarket
London SW1Y 4QX
Tel: 0171-210 4477

Charity Commission
Woodfield House
Tangier
Taunton
Somerset TA1 4BL
Tel: 01823-345000